I've taken tennis lessons from Rob Carver for many years. He is the most positive person/coach I have ever met. When he corrects you, you can feel he's invested in your improvement. He continues to give us more ways and methods to improve. Now as Senior players we realize that Rob isn't trying to make us different players but he helps us become BETTER players. At the end of each session with Rob you feel like a Champion!

—Kathy J.

Coach Rob is the ideal balance of fun, nurturing, no-nonsense taking, skill building and endless upbeat energy! Our kids are fortunate that Rob is their coach!

—Megan S.

Coach Rob Carver taught me the fundamentals of tennis as a junior player, to be competitive as a high school state champion and young adult and now, as a seasoned adult, continues to instill a love for the game. Years later, I get to experience it all over again as Coach Rob teaches my own children a love for the game. From 5 to 95, Coach Rob continues to teach, lead and raise up the next generation of tennis players!

—Casey A.

When I compete I hear Coach Rob's voice in my head. He's helped me be a better doubles player, a tougher competitor, a problem solver and a more positive player. He's also helped me develop off the court. While I haven't done 1 million push ups in ten years like Coach Rob , I have committed to continuing my fitness off the court. Thanks for the drive to continue to be better!

—Frank T

366 DAYS OF TENNIS

366 DAYS OF TENNIS

A TIP A DAY TO IMPROVE YOUR GAME

ROB CARVER

FOREWORD WRITTEN BY TOM GORMAN

Mountain Arbor
Press
Alpharetta, Ga

ISBN: 978-1-6653-0353-8 0 3 0 4 2 2

♾This paper meets the requirements of ANSI/NISO Z39.48-1992 (Permanence of Paper)

To Heather, Ella, and Dean. Thank you for allowing me the time away from you to "serve" others. Heather, you are the most amazing mother! Our kids are great because of you!

To Mom and Dad, my two biggest fans!

In Memory of Nell Carver

FOREWORD
Written by Tom Gorman

I first met Rob Carver in the 90s when we moved to Atlanta from Bermuda Dunes, CA. At the time, he was conducting drills for juniors at our subdivision. After observing a few of his sessions, we decided to entrust our daughters with him and enrolled them in his weekly drills (sometimes daughters don't listen to their dads.) Over the years, they improved greatly and more importantly they continued to really like the game. Both girls went on to play high school tennis at Marist which at that time was the most successful girls' program in the state of Georgia. Thank you, Rob!

Rob has been teaching and coaching for 37 years and from his vast knowledge and experience he has written an encyclopedia of tips. It's with great pleasure that I'm writing this forward for Rob's book, **366 Days Of Tennis**.

This is a compilation of *how and what to do* from his experience of coaching thousands of players of all levels. It's a road map answering any questions you may have…and then some (anyone who mentions Metallica in a tennis book is very evolved).

Rob numbers and titles each stop (day) along the way with a simple word or phrase, and then explains each one in a concise paragraph. When I read his book, I took out my own notebook to jot down some highlights and found I was quickly filling it up. Just a few are: use more lobs, footwork, 'down the middle', volley against a wall, exaggerate during warm up, ball toss, and of course, choosing your partner. All gems and literally hundreds more to help you be a better tennis player!

This is an inspiring, educational, informative, and insightful book. I'd encourage every player at all levels to invest in a copy of **366 Days Of Tennis.**

The title tells it all, because only in Atlanta would tennis players want each year to be a leap year giving them one more day of tennis!

—Tom Gorman Former U.S. Davis Cup Captain

INTRODUCTION

It's been said that success doesn't happen in a day but rather it is a result of what you do daily. Every great athlete has daily habits, rituals, and training methods. Each aspect of their training is a piece within their success puzzle. The mental side of training is often overlooked by amatuer athletes. If you are reading this now, you are the type of player I love to teach. A player that looks for every way possible to improve is the perfect person to read 366 Days of Tennis. You can read one tip a day or several. Feed your brain daily like you train your body. Keep this book in your racket bag and read a tip or two before you practice or play a match. Just like practicing your serve, when you read these tips over and over again, you will gain a mental edge over your opponents. Become like one of the greats and improve in some way, everyday. If you only read one tip a day and utilize it to get better, my mission will be accomplished. The names mentioned in this book are players that I teach and learn from on a daily basis. I'm very blessed to teach so many great kids and adults. The smiles and laughter come easy because of you all! I hope you enjoy 366 Days of Tennis, and I hope it helps you grow as a player.

1 Reach or Run?

A common mistake on an easy ball at the net is to take a big step and reach for the ball. When you take one step you don't have much momentum. Think about what happens when you are driving and have to slam on the breaks: Your momentum stops and the front end of the car goes down. When you take one step on the court, your upper body moves downward which results in your volley landing in the net.

This past week, two strong net players did this. John on Monday night and Jenn on Wednesday morning both reached for their volleys. When they ran to and through their volleys rather than reaching they looked like the great volleyers they are. This past March, Tad and Kelly became better at the net as well. Most passing shots won't be close to you, so logically you will be on the run. You should run through your contact point to keep your upper body moving forward. This will also help you if you have a tendency to volley down rather than forward. Remember to run rather than reach and you will volley like a Champ!

2 The Two Things to Say to Your Partner

Henry and Hayden were playing against Julia and Hailey. It was a fun lesson with four great kids. However, even great kids can get a little too intense during competition. These four learned the two most important things to say to your partner. When your partner wins the point with their good shot simply say, "Good shot!" No need to keep talking… just collect yourself and move on to the next point. Too often players will talk about what a great shot it was and lose focus. When your partner misses a shot, just say, "Nice try!" then move on. The worst thing you can do is to try to correct your partner and fix their mistake. Tell them "Good shot or nice try," then move on to the next point.

This is great advice for all players, juniors and adults.

3 Solve the Problem

Christie hit a sharp crosscourt forehand that pushed Lourdes off the court. Lourdes hit a forehand return but Bettina hit a winning volley between Lourdes and Natasha. Lourdes and Natasha realized that if they gave Christie a drive, she would control the point. On an adjacent court, Lacey and Shayna were playing against Hannah and Elka. Lacey and Shayna realized that Hannah hit a strong out wide serve, which helped Elka poach. Lacey and Shayna changed their return positions so they could return Hannah's serve.

After losing several points, most players just get frustrated rather than asking problem solving questions. "What shot is she hitting that sets up her partner? What shot am I giving her that allows her to hit her potent shot?" When you ask quality questions you get quality answers.

When you problem-solve, you realize how you can change the tempo and hopefully change the score of the match in your favor.

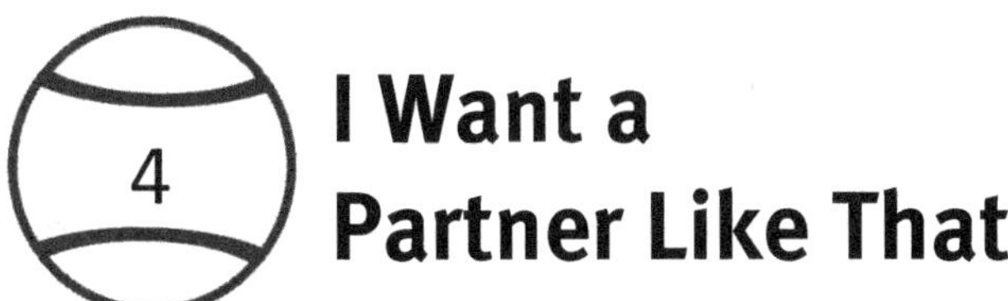

4 I Want a Partner Like That

In doubles, Wendy hit several strong groundstrokes then Judy said "I want a partner like that!" Judy is a strong net player and having a partner with good groundstrokes sets her up. You might have a partner that has a strong serve but doesn't like the net. You on the other hand are good at the net and are able to poach the weak returns produced by your partner's good serves. A good partnership isn't always two strong baseliners or two strong net players. A good team helps each other out by setting each other up and also being steady for each other. Know your partner's strengths as well as their weaknesses.

5 Weather the Storm

What do you do when players like Tom and Shaun are dominating? Both men are tall and hit well off both sides. When they are on, they become more aggressive. We've all played against players that are always on and difficult to beat. Rather than getting frustrated and trying to outhit them, remember to hang tough. You want to weather the storm and stay neutral long enough for them to cool off. Try to slow down the match by playing two-back at the baseline and lobbing more if possible. Players that are on want to continue playing at the same pace or play even faster. Try to hit softer and slower shots so they have to generate all the power. Slower shots also make the points last longer. Do whatever you can to change the rhythm of the match. Players that seem to be human backboards like Dan and Jim understand how to counter punch players that are dominating. It's difficult for anyone to dominate for two hours so do your best to weather the storm.

6 Repeat to Remember

If you want something to stick, do you only say it once? For example, if you want to get more angles out of your shot, and tell yourself to hit the outside of the ball, and it works, shouldn't you say it again and again? Try it the next time you practice. In your mind say the fundamental trigger word that helps you hit the shot you want. Keep your thoughts simple and proactive, then repeat them! *Never* tell yourself something counterproductive like, "Don't miss," or, "Don't screw up!" When you try to avoid something, you tend to get what you're trying to avoid. You might have heard "you get what you think about." Be careful also not to say things like "Win the point," or, "Hit a winner," because these things aren't totally in your control. Tell yourself the way you want to execute and repeat it to yourself again and again until you are confident you can hit the shot you want.

7 Run Around It!

Yes! You can run around your backhand in doubles! Usually, when you picture someone running around their backhand, it's during a singles match. If you're right-handed and on the ad side, you can run around your backhand and use your forehand as a weapon. You can hit your forehand inside out crosscourt or rip it down-the-line. When you rip it down-the-line it doesn't matter if you win the point because the net player has less time to react. When you run around your backhand, the net player will hold their position and forget about poaching your middle shot. This allows you more space to hit a crosscourt shot. Should the net player return your forehand down-the-line, you can then jump on their weak volley with another strong groundstroke.

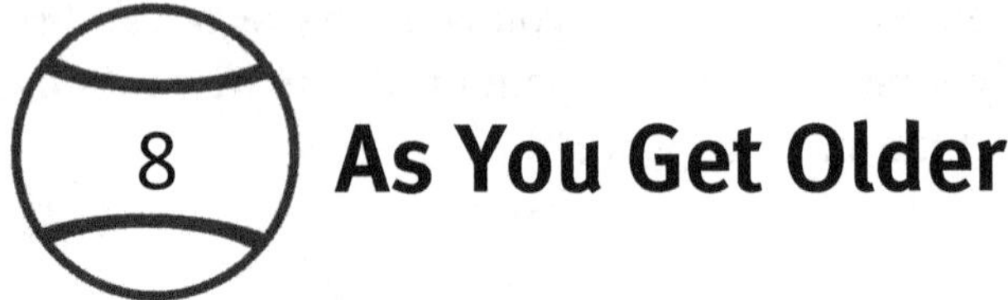

8 As You Get Older

As you get older, you can rely more on your experience rather than your physical skills. When you rely more on your experience, you will become a smarter player. And you will win more! When you can't close in as fast as you used to, you will become better at making a half volley. When you can't turn and leap to reach your opponent's lob because you don't jump as high, you will hit a better approach shot so that they can't lob you as easily. You will also focus more on placing your shots rather than relying on sheer power. You will take pleasure in forcing errors from your opponent as well as making points difficult for them. Play smarter as you get older and use your experience to beat those younger players.

9 Throw a Ball

Do you want a more powerful serve and overhead? To train this skill, start throwing a ball. You could use a junior-sized football, a tennis ball, or play catch with a baseball. Don't worry about how comfortable you feel or how fast you throw. By throwing you are emulating the serving and overhead motion. A good friend of mine that we called Goofy, was a former MLB pitcher. In the offseason, he would throw a football to build up his arm strength. By throwing, you build up strength and flexibility in your arm. Returning to tennis, this will add strength and racket head speed to your serve and overhead.

When you start, just throw twenty or thirty times. If you get crazy and throw one hundred or more you will be very sore the next day. Remember when throwing, you want your arm to be loose and move with a relaxed motion, just like when you serve. One of my players, Jessica, throws a baseball with her sons and if you ask her it pays off in her tennis game. She has a gun for a serve and a lethal overhead. So go get a ball and throw!

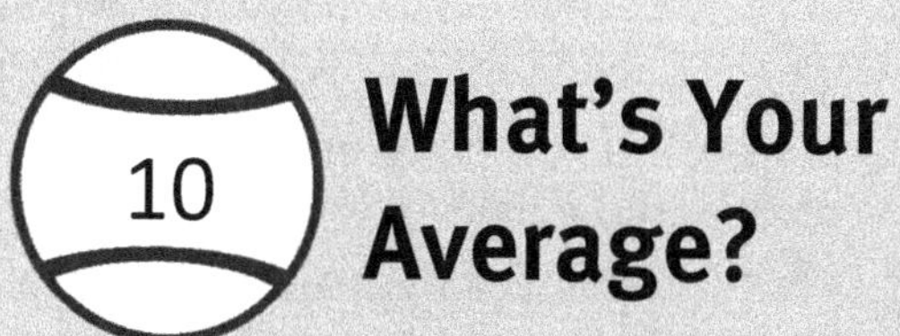

10 What's Your Average?

What is your average of service returns put in play? When you return serve, the goal is to get a high percentage of balls back in play. Unfortunately, most players make the mistake of trying to win the point with the return and then make errors. Think of your return like a baseball player. Rather than trying to hit the unlikely homerun, a smart baseball player will help his team more by hitting a high average like Tony Gwynn or Derek Jeter. Especially when your opponent makes his first serve, you want to reduce your backswing and hit a more controlled return. The higher average of returns in play puts more pressure on the server, and will often lead your opponent to get frustrated and overhit. This will also lead to them missing more!

11 Move Before They Hit.

It sounds so simple, but too many times players wait for the ball to be hit by their opponents before they actually move. Ever watch a professional return serve? They rock back and forth, side to side, or up and down. Some players spin their rackets in their hands and look like they are about to win a sprinting race. They are moving before their opponent serves so that they can be quick to react to the serve. A position on the court that is often neglected is at the service line when your partner is returning serve. Why should you move even when the ball isn't directed to you? You need to be ready in case the next shot comes your way. You want to be on the balls of your feet to react to the potential poach of your opponent's net player as well. After a while, it will become a habit and you will be a better player because of your movement. Remember what Hall of Fame basketball coach, John Wooden, used to tell his players, "Move, move, move!"

12 Lob Up the Stairs

When a player asks how to hit a lob, I always ask them if they have stairs in their house. Picture a straight set of stairs. Now visualize your racket going from the bottom stair to the top of the stairs. As you do this slowly you should see your fingernails if you've opened the racket face (On a groundstroke drive you should only see the top of your hand as you hit). Now bounce a ball next to you and hit a lob as you take your racket up the stairs. Leigh and Bettina are two players that destroy their opponents with their lobs!

13 Whoever Volleys First

Your opponents have less time to react when you volley than when you let your partner hit from the baseline. Your goal in doubles should be to be the first team to volley. You want to take time away from your opponents, as well as make it difficult for them to hit the shot they want to hit. Whoever volleys first, controls the point. You don't have to make a winner on your volley because your opponents are scrambling as you just took time away from them. After you volley, look to pick off the very next shot from your opponent to make it even more difficult for them. Be the first to volley, like Brandy and Clint, and you will control more points.

14 Note to Parents

For your child to get the most out of the lesson, it is best if you are silent. It will be difficult to sit in silence because you want to help, and even more difficult if you also play tennis. But during matches coaching isn't allowed. You want your child to be able to make adjustments, assess the opponents weaknesses, and deal with the pressure of a one on one sport. Your child is receiving directions and instructions from the coach during the lesson. Let your child learn from the coach. I know you want to help but too many voices overcomplicates the lesson. Furthermore, to be brutally honest, your child doesn't want to hear your advice. You just told them to clean up their room, to do their homework, etc. Let them receive the information and advice from the coach. An hour or so after the lesson and away from the courts, ask them what they took away from their lesson and see what they retained.

15 How Do You Practice?

Michael Jordan once said, "I practice as if I'm playing in a game, so when the moment comes in the game, it's not new to me." Even if you're with your buddies having a fun match, remember how you practice is how you play. Stay away from crazy or unrealistic shots that will likely not go in. It's okay to work on different shots because that's how your game grows, but you shouldn't be foolish. Too often when a player has the game point in practice, they relax or try to blast some uncontrollable powerful shot. In a real match, you wouldn't risk your opponents coming back because you were careless on an easy shot. Keep your mental edge and focus in practice and you won't have to find it in a match. Look at any video of Roger Federer practicing as an example. The first thing to notice is his footwork. If you just watched his feet move you couldn't tell if he was playing in a match or practice. There are no switches to turn on just because it's a match. Remember you play like you practice!

The Difference Between Levels

"What is the difference between different levels of players?" asked Darlene, a new player curious about ways to get better. The difference between a C-level player and a B-level player is just one shot. The C-level player is more inconsistent and misses a shot that the B-level player will consistently make. The difference between the B-level player and the A-level player is what they do with that shot. The A-level player has better placement with their shots. The difference between an A-level player and an AA-level player is all about experience. The AA-level player is anticipating where their opponent is returning or hitting their shots. Notice that power is not mentioned.

Yes, the more talented players sometimes hit harder, but winning tennis is about consistency and placement. Focus on making your shot to a specific target then anticipate where your opponent will return your shot… keep it up and your level will go up!

17 The Score Affects People

How do you feel when the score is four-all, deuce? Now consider if you won the first set and you are winning 4-3, ad in? How about if you are down a set and you are receiving the serve, down 40-15, and your opponents are up 4-3? It's natural to think about what could happen *if* you lost or won the next point. To improve, stop thinking about the consequences of winning or losing the point. Instead, play your shots in a high percentage way because of the score. All three of the above scenarios dictate that you play your first shot in a high percentage manner. Also remember that if you are nervous and feel pressure, there's a good chance your opponents are also feeling nervous. Let them think about winning or losing while you embrace the tight score and know that high-percentage is the best way to play in this situation. Furthermore, focus on thinking about a proactive fundamental so that you *do* something rather than trying to prevent a mistake. Both Wendy and Lorrie were clutch today when it was game point because they knew to play high-percentage!

18 Tall Players and Short Players

Both tall players and short players love to show off their range and their quickness. Trying to pass a tall player at the net seems very difficult because of their reach. When you hit towards the open court and the short player scrambles and returns it, you can get frustrated at their foot speed and quickness. A great way to neutralize the short player's footspeed and the range of the tall player is to hit your shot directly at them! The tall player has to get their big body out of the way so that they can reach the ball. The short player can't show off their quick feet because they are trying to move to the side so they can hit. Don't be intimidated by someone's size either! Remember a tall or big person is also a big target. Katherine and Marcia understand how to play against these two extreme players because one is tall with a lot of range and the other isn't as tall, but is very quick and fast.

19 Mini Tennis is Great!

Mini tennis is played only inside the service boxes. In singles, alleys are out and you have to let the ball bounce. Mini tennis is a great game to work on your touch shots, slice shots, drop shots and your creativity. Mini tennis helps you gain racket control and helps you do more with the ball. You will also find a good contact point in relation to your body. Sarah and Pam were perfecting their slice and angled touch shots today when we played some mini tennis. After playing mini tennis you will improve in situations when you have a short ball, a low approach shot, and even when your opponent hits the net and the ball falls short on your side leading you to make a delicate return. Play some mini tennis singles or doubles and you will improve your touch as well as get a great workout in a small space.

20 Anywhere But Here for 2 Hours!

Where is the best place to stand in the service box when your partner is serving? In short, anywhere but the same spot for the next two hours! There is no absolute "best" place to stand. Tennis is a situational sport. When your opponents lob often, you need to stand farther back in the box. If your opponent drives the majority of their returns, you want to stand closer in the box. Does your opponent always hit the same shot? Of course not! So why would you stand in the same spot for every point? Try to stand in a different spot and see how you can influence your opponent's returns. It can also be fun to force an error from your opponent when all you did was stand in a different position.

21 Height = Depth

How do you know if your opponent's shot will land deep or short in your part of the court? New players Lauren and Caitlin were working on their tracking skills today. They realized that there are many clues that a player will inadvertently show you that let you track where their shot will land on your side of the court. A player's racket face, the speed of their swing, and shoulder position are a few indicators about their shot. After you read your opponent's posture you need to read the ball. Off of a groundstroke drive, the higher the ball is above the net, the deeper it will land in the court. Lobs can be hit high but land short in the court. A groundstroke traveling close to the net will land short on your side. Rather than waiting for the ball to cross the net on your side, look at the height of the ball right after your opponent hits it. When you do this you will track and anticipate the depth of their shot earlier and be in a better position to hit your shot.

22 Out in Front, Up on Top

When players make mistakes, they typically say things that won't help them correct their mistakes. "Stop hitting the net! Quit double faulting... Don't swing on your volley... I always miss my overheads." Sound familiar? What is more helpful is to tell yourself what you want to do to execute your shots. This is a double tip to help your toss placement as well as your contact point on your serve. You want to toss out in front of your body. You also want to make contact on top of the ball to get the most leverage possible. When you step up to the baseline to serve, tell yourself, "Out in front, up on top." You will be focusing on what you want, rather than reinforcing your bad habits or mistakes. This has been very helpful for Annie and Holly as they improve their serves.

23 Eyes Up

Your serve is all about rhythm. When you control your toss, you typically have a good serve. A bad toss leads to all kinds of errors and a definite inconsistent serve. When you prepare to toss you should look up. You want your eyes up to where you intend to place your toss. When you watch the ball from the starting position, your eyes and most importantly your head move. When your head moves your vision and balance suffer. Put your hands together then eyes up! Try it!

24 Build a Better Backhand

If you have a two handed backhand and want to make it stronger try this. If you are right handed, your right side is the dominant or stronger side. The problem is that you get the majority of your strength and power from your left side turning through your backhand. Here's how you can build up your left side. Line up as if you're hitting your backhand. Take your right hand off of the grip. Now hit 15-20 left handed shots (this is actually a left handed forehand). At first, you will feel weak; with more repetition you will begin to turn your body. You want to turn your hips and shoulders as you make your one-handed shots. After 15-20 of these, try hitting some two-handed backhands and see how you feel. Then do another twenty, alternating between a one-handed (left hand) then two-handed backhand. You will notice you feel stronger as your unit turn improves.

25 Why?

Hall of Fame band director, Gene Inglis, told me a great story from his days in college. He said his philosophy professor gave them a one-question final exam. The question was: "Why?" The next point you lose in a match ask yourself ,"Why?" More specifically, when your opponent hits a winner, ask why? Do they just have an awesome forehand or did you hit a ball in his strike zone? Do they have a great lob or did you hit your shot straight to them? If you ask "why," you will look for answers to improve your technique. Mistakes leave clues and when you reflect back, you will find them. Debbie realized today why Peggy was hitting winners. Debbie made adjustments on how she hit her next several shots to Peggy so that Peggy couldn't continue hitting her winners. Keep asking why then make your adjustments.

26 Receiving a Ball Hit Right at You

Your opponent either seves right at you or you are receiving a groundstroke that is traveling directly at you. Should you hit a forehand or a backhand? You should hit your strength or your favorite shot. If you're playing singles, you could also choose the shot closest to the outside of the court so that you are moving towards the middle. This places you in a better position to receive the next shot. When you hit your shot directly at your opponent, pay attention and remember which shot they chose. This is a tip off of which shot is their favorite shot or more comfortable shot. Tonight Mike was hitting right at Tom to neutralize his reach. Tom is tall and has very heavy topspin when he is able to extend to hit his groundstrokes. Mike was wicked smart to hit straight at his tall opponent!

27 Who Plays the Middle Shot?

You and your partner are playing two-back at the baseline and your opponent hits a shot down the middle between you. Who is supposed to hit it, you or your partner? Some people say that the forehand should take the middle shots. If you're the ad side player, you might have a better backhand than your forehand. Or the deuce player might have a weak backhand and they don't want to hit their backhand. This is one of those things you need to discuss when you decide to play two-back. The rule that the forehand takes the middle applies more to the overhead than groundstrokes. A forehand overhead is much easier to hit than the backhand overhead. Rick and Paulette were playing two-back tonight and decided who should take the middle before the first point was played. Good thinking by Rick and Paulette!

28 You Don't Have To Hit a Winner

It feels great to hit a winner, but you don't have to hit winners to win! For example, your opponents rush the net together and you have two choices. You could go for a winner, or you could hit a shot that makes it very difficult for them. There's a higher likelihood of them missing your difficult shot, than you hitting an outright winner. The bonus is when they miss they also get mad at themselves for their mistake. Hit a winner if you want but remember you don't have to hit a winner to be successful!

29 Switch Sides After Losing a Set?

You and your partner just lost the first set and your partner asks you, "Should we switch sides?" Before you switch, consider this. The most important thing on a return-of -serve is keeping the return away from the net player. If you're in the middle of a set and your opponent keeps poaching, or you simply can't return crosscourt, you and your partner should play two-back at the baseline. You might have trouble with one of your opponents but return the other server just fine. In that case I wouldn't switch sides. However, if you feel you can't keep the return away from the net player, and you have trouble with both servers, then maybe you should switch sides. Too often players switch when they lose a close set (i.e. 6-4 or 7-5). After switching and losing the match, one may realize they might have been better staying on their side and playing two-back.

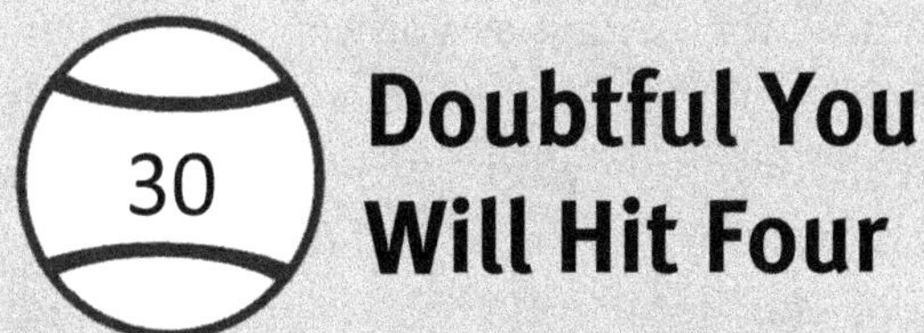

30 Doubtful You Will Hit Four

Here's some good news for those that struggle with consistency. Rarely will you have to make four shots in a row, especially in doubles. When working with Clay on his doubles game, he mentioned that he struggled making four shots in a row. I told him that not many players can. If you feel uncomfortable rallying from the baseline or fear having to hit four in a row, you need to move into the net position. One of the easiest times to move to the net is off of your opponent's second serve. The second serve is usually slower than the first serve, so you have an easier ball to hit your approach shot. When you move into the net you are putting pressure on your opponent. When players feel pressure, they rush their strokes and make more errors. Don't worry about how many shots you have hit. Odds are your opponent won't make four shots so you won't have to either!

31 Quick Hands-Use the Wall

One of the best ways to develop quicker hands is to practice volleying against a wall. In a match, if you hit too hard, you won't have time to continue a rally. Start by trying to volley five in a row. After five in a row, progress to ten and then continue for as long as you can. Next, alternate between forehand and backhand volleys. Here's where you can really improve your quickness. After you get consistent at alternating, go faster and faster until you miss. Keep track of your total and try to make more and more. A good 10-15 minutes will make your forearm feel tight. When this happens, take a break from volleys and serve twenty balls. Now back to the wall and volley some more. Not only do you improve your quickness with this exercise, but you improve your touch and feel.

32 Confidence Booster or Confidence Killer?

You receive an easy ball and you move in towards the net to hit a winner. You unfortunately hit the ball 6 feet out! That's right, you blew it! Join the club!

Every player has missed an easy ball from time to time. The problem is the next easy ball. If for just a millisecond you think about your last screw up, you are in trouble. Don't let one mistake turn into a confidence killer. What you should think about is that you did something well enough to receive an easy ball. You put yourself in position to have the upper hand in the point. When you make the easy shot you feel great. That's a confidence booster. Just keep tunnel vision on the easy shots and execute it.

Stand Where You Want

The only person that is required by the rules to stand in a particular spot is the server. Usually, there will be a discussion after the returner's partner changes positions between first and second serves. The returner's partner will sometimes stand very close to the center service line. Peter is a master of this. He will stand in the middle of his service box until the score is 30-All or deuce. Then he will move very close to the T. Lorrie also did this in a recent mixed doubles match. This is a smart move because the server is distracted by your change of position. When you change your position in a match and your opponents question you, just politely tell them you are fine because you know the rules.

Red Alleys

Nancy was hitting an angled volley today and just missed wide. I told her to volley towards the middle of the service box in the direction of the singles line. She realized that she still had a good angle on her volley when she did this. I told Nancy and her partner Laura to visualize the alleys painted red. Red means danger zone and to be careful. It's ok if your shots land in the alleys. You don't necessarily want to aim for the alleys, just aim for the singles lines. The alleys are only 4 ½ feet wide. Aiming for the singles lines will give you the alley space for cushion.

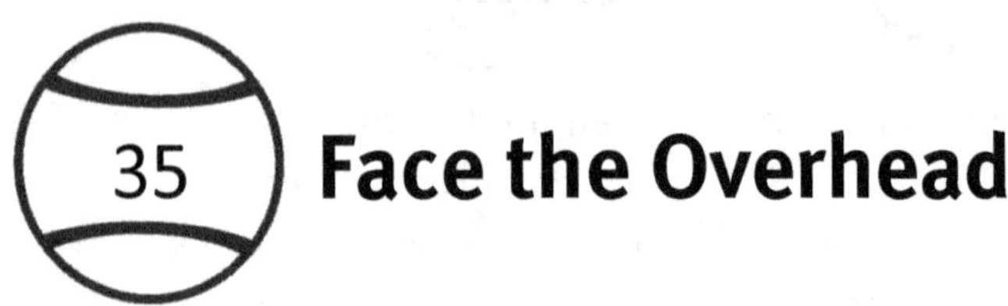

35 Face the Overhead

You're up at the net and your partner hits a short lob. The opposing net player turns and gets ready to slam the short lob. Your instinct is to turn and run so you don't get hit with the ball when that's really not your best play! When you see the net player turn to hit, you should move back. When you see your opponent swing, stop where you are even if you are in no-man's-land. The few feet that you have moved back give you precious milliseconds of reaction time. By facing the overhead, you can now try to block the ball back. Turning away from your opponent gives you zero chance to get the ball back in play. The speed of your opponent's overhead will allow you to block it. Have courage and know that when you get the first overhead back in play, your opponent might get frustrated, over hit, and miss the second overhead.

Anger is Normal

"Hey Coach, what about all that mental toughness stuff you've been talking about?"

I want you to be mentally tough and most importantly mentally tougher than your opponents, but we are all human and anger is normal. Tennis is an emotionally draining sport so just embrace the fact that you're going to get mad from time to time. You should process your anger in the twenty seconds between points. You've heard the advice that when you're really angry with someone to count to 10 before you speak? Well after you lose a point in tennis and feel like blowing a gasket, remember you have a full 20 seconds to let that anger go and move on to the next point.

"I Haven't Hit in Forever"

Everyone will take a break from time to time, but what should your mindset be when you get back out onto the courts? The best way to play is to just enjoy your time while on the court. Enjoy the sheer art of hitting a tennis ball. If you try to be too good or play as well as you did the last time you played, you will be adding pressure to yourself. Naturally you will feel a bit rusty, so just give it some time. Know that the more you hit, the better you're going to feel.

After your first hit, do everything you can to hit within the next couple of days rather than waiting a week.

38 Step On the Gas!

Your opponent hits his approach to you and you have an opening to pass him. Your opponent is also a good mover so you need to hit a strong shot past him. That's right... time to let it rip! A common mistake when trying to add power is to swing fast just using your arm and upper body. However, a great deal of power comes from your legs. This is true for all shots. When you need to pass your opponent, remember what you do when you pass someone on the highway. You put your foot down on the gas pedal. When you put your foot down in tennis you drop down and load your weight. Remember to step on the gas when you want to pass.

39 Whatever It Takes

Former Pittsburgh Pirate, Gino Cimoli, was giving a hitting clinic and mentioned, "I don't care if your butt is facing the dugout, your shoulder is facing the moon....if you are hitting, keep doing what you're doing. Whatever it takes to get it done! If you are hitting well, keep doing what you are doing!" Too often tennis players worry about hitting correctly. There are two players that I am currently coaching that do something rather unique. They are dominant on groundstrokes with their right side but serve better with their left hand. No it's not common, but it works for them… whatever it takes. If you are making shots, winning points, and winning matches, you are doing what you should do.

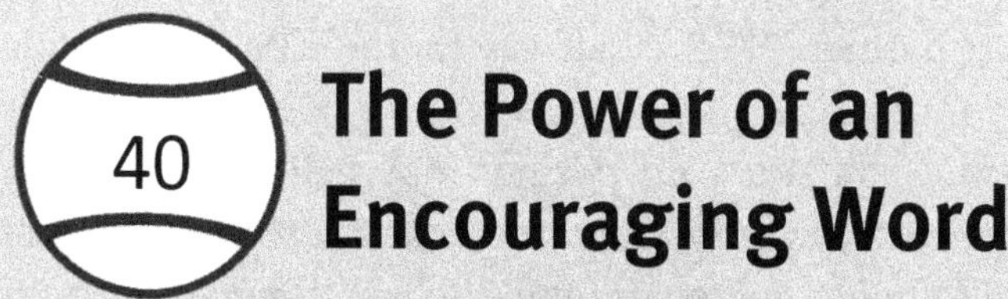

40 The Power of an Encouraging Word

When I was in seventh grade playing baseball for the Angels, I hit the top of the fence in left field which was very close to a Home Run. Coach Jerry Richardson said "Almost, keep it up Carver, everyone hits Home Runs on this team!" Encouragement can come from anyone. Next time your partner does something well, as you high five them, tell them they are a good player. Better yet when they miss, say something like, "Forget that miss, you make the majority of those!" Tell another teammate before they walk on to the court, "Hey, you got this. You and your partner are strong!" Many people play well but don't actually believe they are good players. Am I talking about you? A good word of encouragement can do wonders for everyone. Don't ever forget that! Also one amazing night in July, 1979, I hit a bomb which hit the scoreboard in left field for my one and only over the fence Home Run! Thanks for the encouragement Coach Richardson!

41 The Great Race to 48

At some point in your career, you will win the first set 6-2, 6-1, or even 6-0. Then unfortunately your opponents make an amazing comeback and win the match. In this situation, remember the great race to 48. You need to win a total of 48 points to win a match: 4 points per game x 6 games = 24 points in each set. When you win the first set, tell your partner, "We're halfway there!" The other half is usually more difficult to win as your opponents make adjustments. You and your partner may believe that if you won the first set easily, then the second set should be just as easy. When you are winning, the last thing you should be thinking about is winning. Keep your focus on one point at a time and stay focused. Your goal should be to have a more dominating second set than the score of your first set. Remember to win it's a race to 48!

42 Show Them Your Best Early

If you love your forehand and like to run around your backhand, do it. Do it early. Like to come in on your opponent's second serve? Do it early. If you like to lob over the net player to run the server? Do it early. There's no reason to save your best abilities for the second set or hit it until the third set. You win points with your best and when your opponents see what you can do, they have to change what they're doing. You have the upper hand when they have to adjust to your game. Keep taking advantage of what your opponents give you. Not only should you hit your favorite shots as much as possible, keep going to the well. "The well" is your opponent's weakness. Remember to go to the well until it runs dry and keep hitting them with your best.

43 New Racket

When was the last time you purchased a new racket? If your racket is over five years old, it's time for an upgrade. Even if you buy the same frame that you use now, you will help your game. Racket frames fatigue over time from playing and restringing. You should also try a new type of racket that is new on the market. As you get older you might want to try a larger sized or lighter racket which gives you more mobility. There's no right or wrong when it comes to buying a racket. It's your preference. If you can add something to your game it's always worth trying something new.

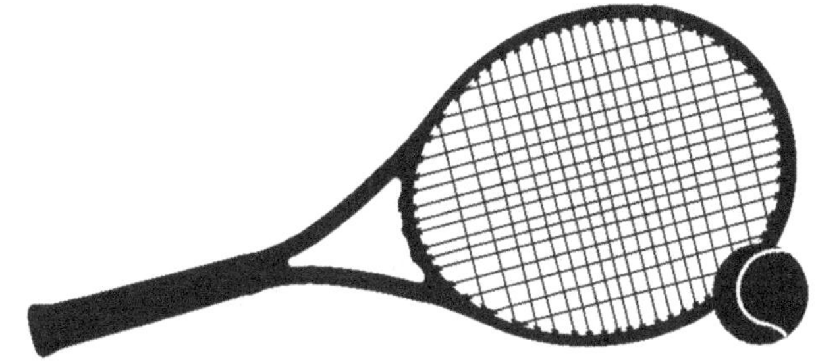

Match Point!

It's match point against you and you are receiving serve. The first thing to do is have your partner come back to the baseline with you. Do everything you can to lob your return of serve and lob it as high as possible. Think about the mindset of your opponents. They are both thinking about the cheers from their fans and the compliments from their teammates for playing such a great match. Everyone gets excited when they are about to win. However, they haven't won anything yet. When you lob to the moon, your opponents have plenty of time. They have plenty of time to screw it up! On easy shots, players often get lazy or overthink things. Do everything you can to make the match last longer and longer. Hopefully your opponents can lose focus just long enough for you to make your epic comeback! Ben and Drew make epic comebacks regularly!

High Energy is Intimidating

If you were playing against a team that had both players furiously moving their feet before the point, what would you think? Do you think they would be slow movers on the court, or quick and explosive players? I want you and your partner to start out your next match doing this very thing. Move back and forth, up and back, and be ready to pounce on the return of serve. After the point is over, high five or fist bump whether you won or lost the point. Then start moving again like you have relentless energy. Do it again after every point. When you change sides and sit down to get water, quickly pop up and take your ready positions and start moving again. You will not only feel quick and alert, but your opponents will definitely notice. This is a sign that you're more engaged and want the victory more!

46 I Want to Be Better

Every player wants to be better. Before you decide how to get better, remember this quote from NBA Head Coach Monte Williams: "Everything good you want is on the other side of hard!" Improvement is difficult. In this quick-fix society we live in, too many players get frustrated when they don't get better or win more quickly. Not all improvement will be physical. If you focus on how you can be better mentally, you will also realize that helps your decision making as well. Ask questions about your strengths and be brutally honest with yourself about your weaknesses. Constantly be curious about what your opponents do well as well as their weaknesses. A current buzz phrase these days is "the process." The process should come with a disclaimer; the process is difficult! Learn from your defeats as they will provide clues and answers on how to improve the next time you play. Remember if it was easy, everyone would do it. Get after it! Embrace the difficult things and keep growing.

47 No Earthquake Moves

If you and your partner were up at the net and I told you I would give $100 to the winner of a foot race to the baseline, would you backpedal or turn and run? Your opponent lobs over you and you just reach up to get the lob. Usually you won't reach the lob and if you do, you won't hit a very strong overhead. I know of five adult players that have fallen by backpedaling rather than turning. These five unfortunate players actually broke their wrists when they fell. One woman fell and broke her wrist in warm-ups! When you don't turn, you can lose your balance and you don't have any reach. I call this the earthquake move. The next time you see a lob, turn to whichever side the lob is traveling over you. Ducky has heard me say this so many times that if she ever forgets to turn she looks at me and says "I know… TURN!"

If You're Not Hitting...

The ball goes away from you and towards your partner. Your opponent also lobs over you. They keep hitting the majority of balls to your partner. Could it be that they have great respect for your game and they think they have a better chance against your partner? Maybe. What should you do if the ball isn't going towards you? Remember to MOVE! It doesn't matter if you go anywhere, just stay up on the balls of your feet and bounce. This keeps you ready for your opportunity to hit. If your partner gets pulled off the court you should also move towards the ball with your partner. Keep anticipating and your chance to hit won't be a surprise to you. Casey and Jenni made some great reaction volley's tonight because even though the first couple of shots went to their partners they kept moving and stayed ready!

Pull with Your Partner

You've probably heard to move with your partner as if you are attached by an unstretchable rope. Here's another way to be a great doubles partner. Pull with your partner. For instance, your partner is at the net and you hit a shot that makes your opponent run off the court which is in front of your partner. Your partner follows the ball as they should. Your partner lines up with the opponent to pick off their shot. You should pull with your partner which will help you get close to the ball. On another point you hit an angled groundstroke and you know that hitting an angle gives your opponent an angle. If you move towards your alley to cover the angle, you are leaving the middle wide open. Pull with your partner and you will close the middle and give your opponent very little space to hit into. If your opponent hits an angle, it travels in front of you which you will most likely reach. Today Leslie pulled with her partner Susan and they closed the middle consistently and covered the majority of the court.

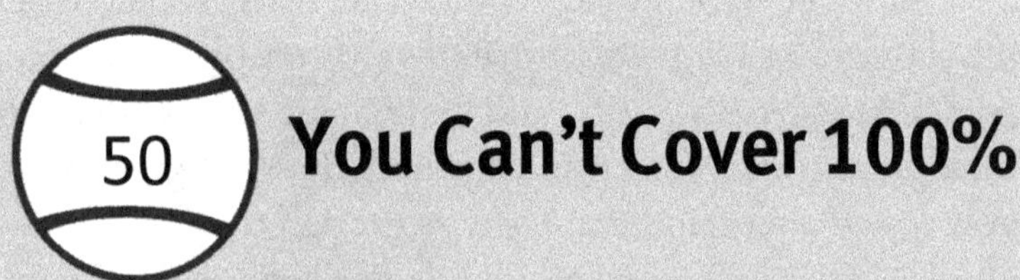

50 You Can't Cover 100%

KJ hit a sharp backhand angle which made Angel run off the court. Angel then hit an incredible backhand down-the-line in the alley past KJ's partner. There were only about two feet of space for Angel to hit into, but she made it for a winner. KJ's partner asked how she could cover that. Unfortunately you can't cover 100% of the court. If your opponent can hit an incredible shot, you just have to give them credit. Also remember how difficult it will be for anyone to hit incredible winners to beat you for two hours! You can probably count the number of incredible shots on one hand so don't let a couple of winners frustrate you.

51 Other Sports

Name another sport besides tennis (golf doesn't count). When you watch other sports you see teams and players change formations and positions the entire game. Oftentimes, they are just trying to get the opposing team to change their strategy. Far too often in tennis players will take the same court position before the point starts. Take the return-of-serve position for example. You currently stand in a place where you are comfortable, but as the match progresses you miss a good amount of returns. Try this when you are missing too much. Stand a few feet to your left or right. The server will wonder what your new strategy might be. When they toss, they will be looking up and then you can jump back to your comfortable spot. Your change of positioning can, and usually will, influence what the server is thinking. Don't get stuck in your comfortable but unsuccessful position.

52 Changing Directions

You could be playing singles or doubles and need to change the direction of the shot instead of hitting back to your opponent, but when you try to hit away from your opponent, you miss too often. Usually the mistake isn't your direction, but it's because you hit too hard. One way to view changing directions is like when you are driving. When you turn, you slow down to maintain control. Think the same way when you are hitting and moving the ball away from your opponents. Focus on control and placement. Power is only a bonus, but not necessary.

53 Chipping the Return

Your opponent hits a hard first serve and you flex your grip, puff out your chest, and try to overpower their big serve. Your return rate when you do this is about 2% in play. It feels as though you have the upperhand when you make it so you continue to do it. Bottom line is it's a losing strategy! Remember Pete Sampras while he was dominating Wimbledon. Pete neutralized many 125 mph serves by chipping or blocking the serves back in play. When you chip a return or block the serve, you don't have to do too much. Keep your backswing very short and focus on getting your contact out in front. You can absorb the pace from the serve and when you return it in play, the pressure goes back to the server. Usually the server will hit your return back with power. Often frustration sets in because they don't expect their big serves to come back.

They Can Miss Too!

In my junior year of college, I was practicing doubles with my partner John. My backhand was on fire but unfortunately my forehand was all over the place. Eventually assistant coach, Jaleel Riaz, had seen enough errors from my forehand and yelled, "Rob! They can miss too! Just get your forehand in and let your backhand do the damage. You don't have to win it... they can miss too!" Too often we believe we need to force the errors with our good shots when we don't have a good shot. An even more difficult strategy is when we try to hit winners that we aren't capable of hitting. Play the ball that's given to you. Realize the shot that you can't hurt them with and just get it in. They can miss too!

"That's Not Going to Beat Us!"

In the 2001 World Series, the New York Yankees took a one run lead over the Arizona Diamondbacks late in game seven. The Diamondback's manager, Bob Brenly, gathered his team on the mound and told them, "That's not going to beat us! We're going to get that run back and get more!" Was Bob crazy? Those were the New York Yankees! The Diamondbacks came back to win the World Series in the bottom of the 9th inning in one of the most epic World Series ever. Now back to tennis. It's 4-5, 30-All, and your opponents scramble for several of your good shots, then finally one opponent hits an amazing winner! They fist bump and their teammates and fans are going crazy. You are now serving 4-5, 30-40, set-point for your opponents. Are you nervous? I want you to look at your partner with strong resolve and say, "That's not going to beat us!" Remember they won one point. You have at least a 50% chance to win the next point. Let the emotions go from the previous point. When you win the next point you are back to deuce.

56 Close the Gap

You receive a short ball and you aren't sure if you should move into the net position. You either aren't confident about your volley skills or you are hesitant because your opponents have strong groundstrokes. If you return the shot and stay back, your opponent has the same amount of space to hit into on their next shot. Think about what could happen if you move into the service box. You could force your opponent to rush his passing shot. They could over or under hit and miss the passing shot. You might have to make a volley which will still put pressure on their next shot. Yes they might hit a winner as well. However, when you move in and your partner is in his service box, there's not much space for your opponent's shot. By moving in, you are taking away a big space for them to hit into. You are closing the gap between the net and baseline. Go ahead and come in and close the gap.

From Average to Above Average

You hit an approach shot that you don't like. You don't like it because you didn't hit a very strong shot. You feel it is weak because it doesn't have much power. How much power do you want? Realize that when you hit with power, you not only risk missing but you are also supplying power to your opponent's passing shot. What you should think is an average approach with little speed and a short depth is actually an above average approach. Your opponent has to move forward to reach your low shot which forces him to lift up. Your shot doesn't have much power, so your opponent has to supply all of their own. Try using a softer and shorter approach and it will drive them crazy that you're not beating them with excessive power.

How Do You Win a Tiebreaker?

Whether you are in the first, second, or third set tiebreaker, you need to remember several things to help you win it. Recall what you and your partner did well when you won each point before this tiebreaker. Also remember where your opponents struggled. Even before you get to a tiebreaker you should be constantly analyzing your opponents for their strengths and weaknesses. Pick on their weaknesses right away and also remember the speed or lack of speed they don't like. Keep making each point as difficult as you can and play high percentage as if every point is a game point. You should never play low percentage shots on game points. Hang tough one point at a time! Let your opponents play the hero shot. You and your teammate will be the victors if you keep your percentages high.

59 It's Amazing What One Move Can Do

What is the one move? It's not a particular move but it is just a move. Alan was at the net while his partner Bob was serving. When the serve bounced in the box, Alan took one step towards the middle of the court. The return of serve traveled through the middle of the court and Alan poached the return. On court two, Scott was returning serve from the deuce side. The opponent missed his first serve, then Scott's partner, Peter, moved one step closer to the T before the opponent hit his second serve. The server looked up when Peter moved and paused, then double faulted. Alan was able to poach because he took one step closer to the middle and Peter forced a double fault just by changing his position by one step. Take one step out of your comfort zone in the next match and see how it can affect your opponents. It's amazing what one move can do!

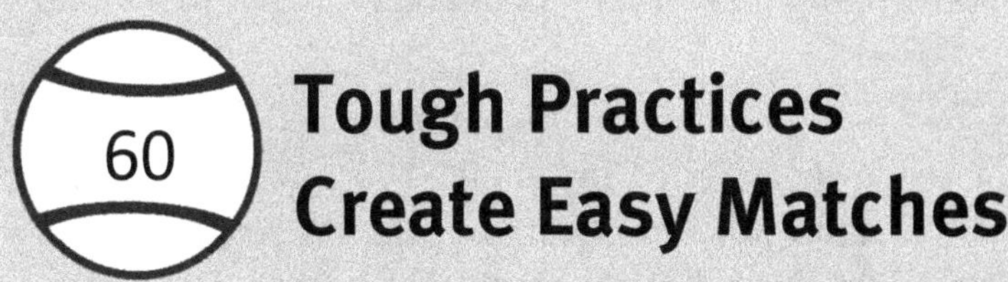

60 Tough Practices Create Easy Matches

I often put conditions on players during practice. Players are awarded bonus points for succeeding, but lose multiple points for mistakes. It might seem unfair but it makes players mentally tougher during their matches. For example, if you missed in the net you lost two points. If you poached the first ball and won the point, you earned three points. Katie was a poaching machine tonight. Jess was hitting sharp angles with big topspin which helped Katie poach. Their opponents were their teammates. Kathy and Robin, who also became more bold at the net because they knew they could score three points. No one at practice liked missing in the net because it hurt when they lost two points. The good news is in a match all points are only worth one, but you become mentally tougher because of the conditions placed on you in practice.

61 Move Through Your Slice

Too often players miss a slice in the net. Missing in the net is the worst error in tennis. You always want your opponents to have to do something. When players miss the slice it's usually because they stop their feet and just work the upper body. You need momentum from your legs to help push the ball to the other side of the court. You can even just walk through your slice. There's no need to be in a hurry as the spin of the slice breaks the rhythm of the rally. Just remember to move through your slice like any other shot and have fun driving your opponent crazy!

62 I Didn't Mean to Hit Such a Good Shot!

Sounds like a good problem, right? Lately Ceci and Liz have been working on their backhands. Ceci has a beautiful one-handed topspin backhand as well as a slice. Liz has a strong slice and has been working on her two-handed topspin backhand. Both players hit great backhands and said something to the effect of, "I didn't mean to hit such a great shot!" What I explained to them was that they had big targets to aim for. When they aimed for the bullseye but didn't hit it directly, they still hit into a good target zone. Players that try to hit the lines or in the alleys often miss because their target is too small. Another reason Ceci and Liz were making good shots is because they were focusing on making shots to a target rather than trying to win points. Give yourself big targets to make your shots and your percentages will go up!

Guessing Leads to Anticipation

Carli hit a sharp crosscourt forehand that made Stephanie run off the court. Brittany moved towards Stephanie in hopes of poaching Stephanie's shot. Carli and Brittany need to know where Stephanie will hit her shot. Because Carli hit a crosscourt shot, she should anticipate a crosscourt return and Brittany will cover a down-the-line shot. Brittany is in position to cover down-the-line but she is also assuming Stephanie will hit it crosscourt because it's the higher percentage play. No one other than Stepanie knows where she will hit, but you should always guess where your opponent will hit their shots. As the match progresses you will pick up on your opponents tendencies and get yourself in a better position to cover their shots.

64 SH*T but Not SORRY!

KJ tried to poach April's return but missed. KJ turned to her partner, Betty, and said "Sorry." Sorry is a bad word. What happens the next time KJ misses? Is she now twice as sorry? What about her third miss? No one likes to miss and let their partner down, but when you apologize to your partner you feel bad for a second time. The problem is that you become hesitant to make the same shot in fear of missing. I told KJ that you can say, "sh*t" but not "sorry." She laughed and gladly took my advice. A mistake isn't a reason to apologize in tennis, just move on to the next point.

65 Hit It Hard!

When working with juniors, especially those under 10 year old, I notice something happens when they keep score. Instead of playing carefree they become tentative. (Adults do it as well!) No one wants to lose, so players pull back and play too cautiously. When I was working with Ella, Will, and Santiago today I told them, "For the next 2 games, hit it hard when you have an easy shot!" Yes they missed a few, but what they learned was how hard they could hit before losing control. Try it the next time you play a practice set. Go for your shots without the thought of missing. Hit freely with the expectation that the ball is going in. You will soon develop the feel for how hard you can hit and still be consistent.

Make Them Struggle

Tennis isn't a game about winning, rather it's a game about losing. Seventy percent of the points at the professional level are ended by a mistake. Today Pat was working on hitting a slower ball to take pace away from her opponent. Debbie, who has a strong backhand, was slicing her backhand rather than hitting her drive. Both Pat and Debbie were hitting shots that their opponents didn't like. Sarah told me she likes to hit soft returns low to her opponent's backhand when she plays singles. Finding shots your opponents struggle with increases the number of errors they will make. Give them slower shots, slice more, hit loopy high bouncing shots mixed with your drives and you will drive your opponents crazy. When your opponents make errors, not only do they get frustrated, but you win!

Loosen Up and Hit Up

When players are trying to hit more topspin, they often swing with a stiff arm and try to muscle the ball. When players like Brian and Kyle miss shots long, they are hitting straight rather than hitting upward which adds topspin. When they loosen up their swings and hit up, they get more topspin on the ball. You can do the same! When you realize you are getting more topspin you can be even more aggressive. Just remember hitting a tennis ball effectively is a timing element rather then, your physical strength. Loosen up and hit up!

It's the Contrast That Kills Them

The majority of players believe that powerful shots win most of the points. If you hit the majority of your shots with power, you risk missing too much and your opponents get used to the speed of your shots. Players like Rick and Paulette have strong and powerful forehands. What wins for both of these players isn't always the strength of their forehands. They both hit softer backhands that are well placed, but not hit with much power. Varying the pace of your shots often drives opponents crazy. Just when they get used to the speed of your shots, you change speeds and break their rhythm. Keep your opponents off balance and remember it's the contrast that kills them!

Line = Line

The majority of shots travel crosscourt in doubles and singles. Crosscourt is the higher percentage direction because there is more space to hit into and the net is lower in the middle. But when should you hit down-the-line? The mistake in hitting down-the-line happens when you attempt to hit down-the-line from behind your baseline. It's more of a distance issue than your skill. Your opponent at the net has too much time to react when you hit from behind the baseline. The net is also six inches higher over the alleys. However, when you are inside the baseline, you can hit an effective down-the-line like Janet. She has a very strong forehand and when she hits from inside the baseline, the opposing net player has less time to react. Just remember if you cross the baseline and are close to the singles or doubles line it's ok to hit down-the-line. Line = line.

Cat and Mouse

For most recreational players, the second serve can be an opportunity for the returner to be aggressive. Often the returner will hit an aggressive down-the-line return past the net player. When you are the server's partner remember the concept of cat and mouse. You are the server's partner and your partner is hitting their weak second serve. Standing still and waiting for the strong return of serve is a losing strategy. Move, fake, or change your position, or any move you can make before their return of serve. This will distract the returner from having an easy return and they will be more focused on your movement rather than making their return. Sometimes it is even effective to stand near the middle of the court and when the serve lands, you jump back towards your alley. This move will distract the returner. Have fun with your movement and bluff the returner into focusing on you rather than hitting an easy return.

Be a Ball Hog!

You poached so what do you do now? Poach again! But what if you go across the middle on to your partner's side to get the ball? If you are poaching you are making the correct play. If you are poaching and winning the point you are helping your partner win as well. Should you ever have a partner that calls you a "ball hog," thank them! Poaching and making the point difficult for your opponents is always the right play.

72 Tempo Helps Your Timing

Players like Holly that have musical backgrounds understand what tempo is. Tempo is the speed at which you are performing your skill. If you want better timing, think about slowing down your tempo. When you slow down, you tend to relax more and have better balance. When your timing does improve, you feel like you are flowing into your shots with rhythm rather than being stiff and rugged. Remember tennis is about timing and rhythm, not strength. Control your timing with a smooth tempo and you will improve both your control and consistency.

73 Same Ol' Situation (S.O.S)

Any Mötley Crüe fans reading this? How about that song Same Ol' Situation? It's a great song but the S.O.S. in tennis is an unfortunate situation. Too many players stand in the same spot because that's where they are comfortable.

If you stand in the same spot, your opponents get comfortable with where you are and they can strategize against you. When you stand in different positions and give your opponents different "looks" they will think differently. This also works well when you are returning serve. When the score is 30-All, deuce, 30-40, or 40-30, move two steps away from where you started the last point. This move makes your opponents consider why you aren't in the same ol' situation. If you're uncomfortable where you are standing you can move back to your spot when the server looks up to toss. Just remember when your opponent sees something different, they think differently. This is a much smarter way to play instead of being in the same ol' situation.

Beware of the Teaser

Your opponent is on defense and they hit a high ball towards you. You are coming in to take it out of the air because you don't want the ball to bounce high and push you back in the court. This high ball is called the Teaser because, although it's high, it isn't high enough for you to play an overhead. When you hit it, it will be around head level and not an overhead. Tonight Megan and Lisa played the teaser like seasoned pro's. Another difficult part of the teaser is when you aren't inside the service box. You need to play a safe shot unless you get closer to the net. The best way to handle the teaser is to block or volley the ball out of the air rather than swinging at it. By taking your opponent's teaser out of the air instead of letting it take a high bounce you are taking time away from your opponents. This will most likely put you on the offensive for the next shot.

75 It Doesn't Say U.W. It Just Says W!

We all know what "W' stands for... WIN! So what is U.W.? U.W. stands for "Ugly Win". I will take either one and I bet you will too. On court this morning with Cathy, Kathy, and Susan they all won points where they discounted themselves because they hit "ugly" shots. Usually we hit ugly shots because our opponents put us on the defensive. So how should you play on defense? You do what you can to get the ball back in play. If you happen to hit a less than desirable shot or an ugly shot just remember that you got the ball in and that's the name of the game. You don't get bonus points for hitting a "pretty" shot either. Just Win Baby, Win. (There's your Raider shoutout Hanna and Alkire!)

76 "You Hit Differently Every Time You Play"

This advice comes from former pro and current professional coach, Tom Gullickson. Every time you play, you hit differently. On days you are hitting below your normal level, you need to focus on playing smarter. Smarter simply means hitting higher percentage shots and being more controlled rather than playing aggressively. On days when you are playing well, you can be more aggressive. The key is understanding that you can win even on days that you aren't hitting well. You achieve this by constantly focusing on where your opponents struggle and make mistakes. Tom has a twin brother, Tim, who was Pete Sampras's coach and gave him the same advice. "When you don't have your A game working, take off your white collar, put on your blue collar and get to work!" I think that advice worked pretty well for Pete and it can work for you too!

77 Warm Up Speed

Think about how hard or soft you hit the ball in your warm up. The purpose of your warm up is to scout your opponents and warm up, not to hit winners. Most likely you save the hard or powerful shots for when the opportunity arises during the match. If you assess the percentage of hard shots you hit in, versus the percentage of balls you put in play during warm ups, you'll realize you make more shots in warm ups. You aren't trying to win, you are trying to warm up and make shots. Think about a baseball pitcher warming up his arm before he pitches. Save the hard and powerful stuff for when you are totally warmed up. Players like Debbie, Suzy, Susie, and Kim understand how to slow their shots down to warm up speed during their matches when they need to win crucial points. Rather than trying to win a point with powerful shots, hit the warm up speed and make more shots and you will actually win more too!

78 "Why Do I Practice This?"

Mattea yelled this when she missed her backhand lob. She didn't like that her lob was hit too short. What Mattea felt was that she was trying to practice a bad shot because she didn't execute it very well. The shot that drove Mattea deep in the court was a backhand that Pam hit. Pam has a strong backhand and this particular shot was low and hard. Lobbing was the best option for Mattea, as she was hitting a defensive shot. Often we don't hit the shot we want to hit because the one we received was uncomfortable. The important thing to remember is that you need to find a way to get the ball back in play anyway you can when you are on defense. It's okay to practice the defensive shots because at some point you will need to use them in a match.

79 The Magic Pill

Entrepreneur Gary Vaynerchuk once said that if he could give every entrepreneur a magic pill, it would be a pill of self awareness. When it comes to self awareness, I refer to what Hall of Fame basketball coach, Bob Knight, often told his players, "Do what you do well and stay the hell away from what you don't do well!" Too often we as tennis players force shots that we don't have. You might have a powerful forehand and just an average backhand. If that's the case, realize it and be okay with it. You need to be aware of your strengths and weaknesses. Mistakes come when you try to make your backhand as strong as your forehand. Your backhand may never be as strong a shot as your forehand. Players like James and DT are very aware of their strengths and weaknesses. They don't need a magic pill and neither do you. Focus on keeping your weaker shots in play and let your stronger shot dictate play.

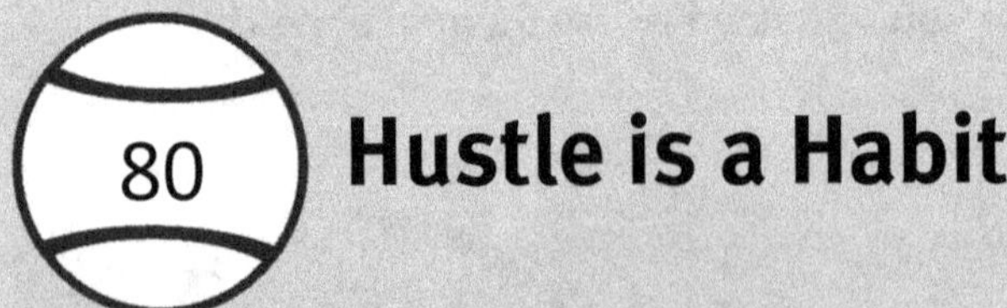

80 Hustle is a Habit

Three of my junior players, Rohan, Will, and Samuel are all very good swimmers. Unfortunately, swimming doesn't transfer to helping quick movements on the tennis court. At the beginning of every lesson the boys do scissors which is a quickness drill to improve footwork. We also practice hustling for *every* ball. They understand that hustling isn't like a light switch. From the first ball in warm ups to the last ball in a match, you should hustle. Sounds easy but all players tend to get lazy. Make it your goal to have your opponent say at the end of your match, "I've never played someone who hustled so much for every shot!"

81 Step Out

You are serving from the ad side in a doubles match against Nancy and her partner. Nancy hits a backhand return which pushes you off of the court. The good news is that you have an angle to return off of her shot. The bad news is that you have been pulled off the court hitting a running backhand. A running backhand is a challenging shot as it's more difficult to hit down-the-line. The best way to handle the angled backhand without changing your serving position is to serve and step out towards the alley. You have time to step out after you serve. Judy does this very well. She serves and steps out behind the alley. This gives her time to get to her backhand without having to hit it on the run. Judy also has time to run around her backhand and hit a forehand. She can hit an inside out forehand or disguise her forehand and drive it down-the-line. Serving and stepping out can give you many opportunities such as a down-the-line drive or inside out forehand.

82 Take It Out of the Air

Your partner lobs the opposing net player which forces them to switch sides. When the baseliner gets to the lob, they are most likely to lob it back to you because they are on the defensive. When the baseliner moves back, you should move into the service line. Then you can volley or hit an overhead off of their lob. The main benefit to taking the lob out of the air is that you take time away from your opponent for their next shot. You also prevent their lob from bouncing high and pushing you back in the court. When your opponent hits a lob or high shot, remember to move up and take it out of the air. You'll be glad you did and your opponent won't!

83 Bounce on the Bounce

Too often players are late getting to the ball. It's usually not because they are slow, but rather because of bad footwork. The most important step in tennis, and many other sports, is your first step. To create a quick first step, remember to bounce on the balls of your feet when the ball bounces on your opponent's side of the court. This will help you push off quickly. Just bounce on the bounce everytime and your quick first step will become a habit. If you want to see quickness in action, come watch Brian and Danny pounce on their volleys.

84 Baseballs and Medicine Balls

Don't worry, we're not talking about off court training. Imagine you are at the baseline and your opponents are up at the net. Your natural instinct is to hit a hard passing shot. The problem here is that there's not much space between them to hit a winner. Your better option is to hit it directly at either player to jam them into making an error with their volley. Here's where you can get into trouble with a hard shot. To begin with, you lose control when you hit hard. Secondly, a straight hard shot will ricochet off your opponent's racket because of the sheer speed. This is like throwing a baseball very hard and fast. The velocity keeps the ball on a straight path. Now consider if you hit with heavy topspin like Mike, DL, or Saban. The heavy spin drops rapidly and also feels heavy for the volleyer. Imagine yourself five feet away from someone and they toss a medicine ball to you. Even though it wasn't thrown at you very fast, the ball is difficult to catch because of its weight. So when you are facing two players at the net, remember to hit a shot with heavy topspin directly at them. They will feel a very heavy ball dipping downward that creates a difficult volley.

Right or Wrong... Commit!

You're up at the net and your partner is serving. The return comes across the middle and you can see the spin of the ball as it passes you. The next game you are returning serve and the serve is short. You move close to the service line to return, but retreat to no-man's-land because you don't know if you should move in. Rather than competing, you are being indecisive. Indecision feels terrible. In addition to feeling lost, you are letting your partner down. In tennis you need to go with your gut. Make your decision and follow through with it. Players like Nicolette and Bettina poach when the opportunity is there and attack when they get the short ball. Keep your thoughts simple and your actions bold and decisive!

Make Them Frantic

How do you feel when you are running off the court to hit a low shot? Calm or frantic? You are running fast and the ball is very low to the court. Your opponents have also closed in and are both at the net. Beyond the physical challenges you are facing, you also have the mental pressures. The score and the possibility of losing the point make your shot even more challenging. Before you think about winning, think about how to put your opponent in the same situations. Leigh and Melanie are great at making their opponents feel frantic. They hit short angles to run their opponents off of the court and lob over the net player to make the baseline player run to the other side of the court. Placing your shots to the open court forces your opponents to move and gives you a bigger space to hit into. Forget about winning with your shots and just think how to make them run and feel frantic.

87 Go Fast to Slow Down

That was a statement made by my player, Holly, in just her fourth lesson! She quickly learned the importance of getting to the ball quickly then slowing down to make the shot. As a player you want to speed up your legs so you get to the ball early. Being early to the ball lowers your stress level and gives you a better chance to be balanced when you hit. You can also plan where you are hitting. Remember to go fast with your feet then slow down to hit.

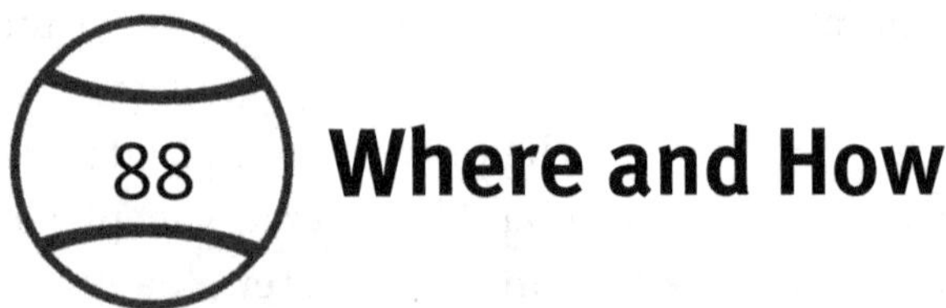

88 Where and How

Where is your opponent hitting the ball? It's not always where you hit to your opponent that forces the error, but rather how you send it to them. Do you hit it low, high and loopy, or do you make the mistake of hitting it waist-high so they are too comfortable? When your opponent makes an error, remember the position they were in and what type of shot you sent them. Think in terms of where and how.

89 The Fun of Learning a New Shot

You may have powerful topspin on your forehand, but can you slice it? After you hit your strong forehand a few times, don't you think your opponents are preparing for a strong shot the next time you hit your forehand? Wouldn't it be nice to get your opponents off balance? This is where you can add some fun to your tennis development. Players like Missy and Liz have great slice backhands. Their slices cause trouble for their opponents. In the last several months they have been working on learning a two-handed backhand. At times the learning curve can be frustrating, however, it can be very rewarding when you see results. Think about learning a new shot like putting another tool in your tool chest.

90 You *Never* Have to Win

Isn't winning the goal? Of course it is. To win you have to earn more points than your opponents. Understanding how you win is the key to winning consistently. About 70% of the points at the professional level are ended by a mistake. So what is the percentage on the recreational level? Definitely more than 70%! To create errors from your opponents you should focus on the shots that are most difficult for them. As you return your opponent's shots, focus on making your shot to its intended target rather than winning the point. When you take the focus away from winning, you actually play with more consistency, which leads to your opponent making more errors which helps you win!

91 The Vets Have Touch

Have you ever played someone with great touch on their shots? Touch is the ability to place the ball by controlling the speed and direction of the shot. I teach some Veteran players or "vets" that have some crazy touch. Bob, Peter, Scott, Al, and Dean all win many points because of their great touch. A funny thing happens when you play tennis for many years. You learn that it's not the speed of your shots that matter most, but instead it's the placement of your shots. The good news is that you don't have to be an experienced vet to have touch. Next time you receive an easy ball at the net, try touching it to a particular spot rather than hitting it hard. You'll be amazed at how much control you can get on the ball.

Hands to the Ball

One of the biggest mistakes with volleys is swinging. The reason many players swing at volleys is because they learned groundstrokes first. Groundstrokes begin with a shoulder turn. When I see players swinging on their volleys I redirect their focus to trying to execute the stroke correctly. I asked a player of mine, named Peggy, if she learned volleys or groundstrokes first. She said groundstrokes. I took her to the service box and had her catch a few balls that I tossed her. I asked her how she caught the balls and she said, "I put my hands out to the ball and caught it." To make your volleys compact and controlled, rather than swing, remember to take your hands to the ball. Your racket will then be out in front and you can place or touch your volleys wherever you want.

93 Show Them Your Strings

Billie Jean King was one of the best volleyers on the ladies tour. She once said, "Your racket should be at eye level *after* you volley." This helps you keep your actions short and compact on the volley. I cringe when I hear a pro or player say the volley is a short stroke. When you say "stroke," the typical result is a swing and volleying isn't a swing. To help control your racket and get the direction you want on your volleys, make sure your opponents see your strings after you volley. Have your strings point to your target before you volley to improve directions.

94 WORDS!

Have you ever missed an easy shot? Have you ever missed an easy shot by four feet? Or you read your opponent's return of serve and poach only to volley straight into the net? What can you say or scream when you miss? DL and Danny yell, "WORDS!" when they miss. I wish I could say I have such restraint. I'm constantly learning from my students. "WORDS" is a great way to blow off steam and still show some class!

95 It's Okay to Do What You Just Did!

You're in the service box and your opponent lobs the ball towards the sidelines. The ball keeps drifting closer to the alley. It goes over your head, and for a split second, you think the ball is going out. The very next second you think it might land in. Should you hit it or let it go? If you let it go and it's out, you win the point. But what if you are wrong and the ball lands in? Wouldn't you feel terrible to lose that point? Today Michele was in the same situation. So what did Michele do? She hit the lob out of the air before it could land. The point lasted several more shots before she and Peggy won the point. After the point Michele said, "I'm not sure if it was okay to do what I just did?" I explained that it's better to play the lob that you're not sure about because once you let it go, you have no chance to hit it after it lands.

96 Stink Today, Shine Tomorrow

How come some days you are good and some days you are really, really bad? In the weeks and days leading up to a match we all practice different strokes and strategies. We get better and can see improvement in our games. And then it happens… your last practice before your match you are awful. That's right, you flat out stink! Then the anxiety sets in. You feel like you're going to be terrible again tomorrow during your match. Here's where you need to understand that it's actually a good thing to stink in practice. When you are practicing, you have thoughts about your future matches and performance. We tend to believe that if we miss in practice, we will also miss during the match. The best strategy when you stink during practice is to flip it around in your mind. Tell yourself that you'd rather stink today than tomorrow in the match. During your match remember that you've put in the practice time and then just focus on your opponent's strengths and weaknesses. Remember that the ball doesn't know if you're at practice or a match. Today is a new day so forget about yesterday and go out and compete.

Mixed Doubles Solution

Mixed doubles or mixed troubles? It really depends on the day and your doubles partner. Returning the serve in mixed doubles can be a challenge. During one practice match with couples Susan and Casey and Brian and Cindy, I noticed that Susan and Cindy were not used to the frequent speed that their male opponents used in their serves. After Brian served, Susan was late with her return, setting up an easy volley for Cindy. A good solution for this would be to play two-back at the baseline. Ladies have told me men decline their request to start two-back because it's too defensive. It is defensive, but the male partner isn't doing anything when the opposing net players are poaching either. Two-back at the baseline gives both players more time to react to aggressive net players and also cuts off the easy middle volley. After the return of serve the male player might go to the net or he might stay back at the baseline. Either way, he isn't a liability up at the service line if or when the other team has an easy volley. After mastering two-back, these couples became even better mixed doubles teams!

98 What's *Your* Tennis Legacy?

That's a big question, right? Think about it for a second. What do you want people to say about your tennis game? Don't think about just your teammates and your friends that see you play all the time. Also consider what your opponents will say about you at the end of the match. Do you want them to say you are erratic? That you are very emotional or can only handle one speed? Or how about they say you were the most consistent player they've ever played? Or that you were the most active net player they ever competed against? Even better for them to say that they never could tell if you were up and down emotionally. The next time you aren't having a good day, forget the score and have the resolve to say to yourself, "When this is over they are going to feel like this was the most difficult match they have ever played." Make it your goal in every match you play, your opponents will have to respect your intensity, your competitiveness, and your grit!

Your shots may come and go but your competitive level will always be high.

HIGHER

You never miss a shot in the net. I want you to remember to hit the ball *higher* when you are on defense or hitting a lob. Even if you hit a lob too short, you want to at least hit it high. A high lob will still give your partner at the net time to retreat before your opponent slams. Tracking a high lob can be tricky for your opponents. Remember on defense you *never* miss. You should always make your opponents hit another shot. Hitting higher more frequently gives your opponents too much time to think and they might even miss your easy shot.

Tempo: Good or Fluid?

One of my players, Steve, is great at controlling his shots. Prior to taking up tennis, Steve played piano and saxophone. As a musician he understands tempo. Too often, when trying to hit slowly or focusing on control, players stop their swing too short and fail to complete the follow through. The result is a stiff, rigid-feeling shot, rather than a smooth and effortless motion. I asked Steve about his tempo as he hit and he said, "I focus not just on keeping a good tempo before the hit, but maintaining a fluid tempo all the way through the hit." BRILLIANT! Whether you are trying to hit with power or hit softly, remember that you want a fluid tempo. The feeling of hitting a good shot should be fluid and almost effortless. Whenever you don't have the feeling of striking the ball well make sure you hit with a fluid tempo.

101 Different Grips

The typical forehand grip is the Eastern grip. The Semi-western grip is great to see if you could hit more topspin. Have you ever been really crazy and tried a full Western grip? If you want to hit a good slice or drop shot the Continental grip will work best. Try changing your grips to see what different spins and shots you can create. There will likely be an uncomfortable adjustment because it's different, but it can add some variety to your game so it's worth the struggle! Just like my Mom told us as kids when we were told to eat a new vegetable, "Try it! You just might learn to like it!"

Play the First Point Like It's the Last

During the French Open of 2021, former World No. 1, Jim Courier, mentioned an amazing statistic. When Rafael Nadal wins the first point against his opponent's serve at the French Open, he breaks serve ⅔ of the time. When his opponents win their first point, they win the game 70% of the time. Now consider how important the first point of each game can be in your matches. Winning the first point gives you the confidence that you're going to win the game whether you are returning or serving. Consider turning up your focus on the first point as if it were deuce or a game point. Try it and you may start winning more!

Your Strength is in Your Struggle

We all have our preferred style of play and hope that our opponents don't figure out our weaknesses or limitations. But is that what the great players think? NO! The great players understand that overcoming weakness in their games is the pathway to greatness. The great ones don't avoid challenges or uncomfortable styles of play, but rather they seek them out. Hate playing players with a lot of spin? Ask your coach to feed you with a bunch of spin. Don't like backhands? Hit as many backhands in practice as you can. Are you uncomfortable serving and volleying? Serve and volley everytime you are winning 40-Love or 30-Love. It's not easy to learn and improve a new skill, however, going through the learning curve and adding to your game helps you deal with obstacles and different styles of play. By practicing difficult shots in practice, you will gain confidence that helps you in a match.

104 Always Be Curious

Why are they such a good player? How do they hit that shot? Why do they win so much when they hit like that? Basketball and baseball were my two main sports before I became dedicated to tennis. It bothered me to see guys play better tennis than me when I was a better basketball or baseball player than them. Why were they better? To this day I am curious about my opponents. You can't judge a good tennis player by his physical appearance or just the way he hits. Being curious is scouting your opponents strengths and weaknesses. When I watched a player that was better than me, I tried to pick up at least one aspect of their game and incorporate it into my own.

105 50/50 is the Wrong Mindset

You are up at the net and your partner is serving. The serve goes to your opponent's forehand on the deuce side. Which direction do you think the return will travel? It will likely travel crosscourt which is the higher percentage play. If the returner is close to the alley and inside the baseline, the return might go down-the-line. So how should you approach this situation if you don't know for sure? The worst mindset is 50/50. You aren't anticipating anything in particular and are at the mercy of the returner. Go with your gut and have a 70/30 mindset. Think in terms of "probably" instead of "maybe." As the match progresses, you should get a read on where they like to hit. If your opponent is hitting any shot other than a return, try thinking like this. If the ball is to your right, assume it will be returned on your right side. If you're wrong and it travels to your left it will travel in front of you. Remember if you guess wrong, no one knows what you were thinking. Keep guessing and it will soon lead to anticipation. A 70/30 mindset is proactive which helps you to commit to playing your shot rather than simply being reactive to your opponent's shot.

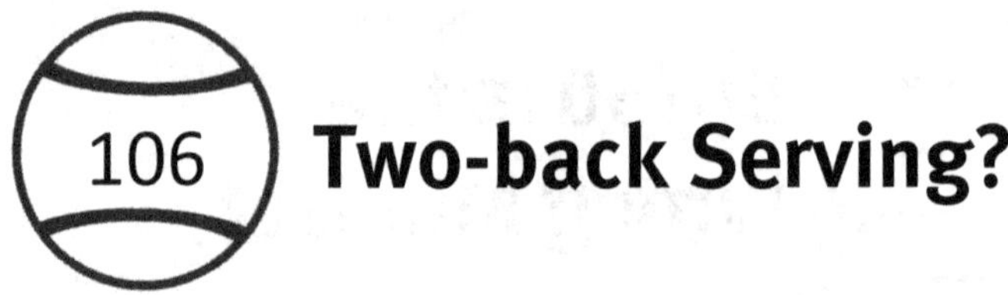

106 Two-back Serving?

You've likely returned serve with you and your partner back at the baseline, but have you ever *served* in the two-back formation? Isn't it better to have a partner up at the net so they can poach? Most of the time, yes. However, if the returner has a great lob or your partner is uncomfortable up at the net, serving two-back is actually smarter. During one practice, Leigh, Christi, and Jenn were having a tough time covering Bettina's lobs up at the net. Even when they started at the service line, her lobs pushed them deep into no-man's-land. For the returners, something even more frustrating is switching to cover a deep lob because the bounce is so high. Jenn stayed at the baseline when Leigh was serving and while Bettina could still lob, Jenn and Leigh kept the lobs in front of them longer. Christi said, "If my opponent is hurting me with a lob I like to go back too." Like any shot that is hurting you in doubles, changing formations is a smart way to influence your opponent to change their game.

107 The "Go To"

During the warm up your focus should be on your opponent's strengths and weaknesses. Usually your opponent will hit their preferred shots when the ball is hit directly at them. Watch them when they are at the net and pay attention to their body language. You can usually spot the more aggressive player based on how many volleys they ask for. If they only play a few volleys, they probably don't like to volley. You need to be able to go to your partner at the end of the warm up and tell them what weaknesses you saw in your opponents. After your partner shares their information with you, the two of you will know who the "Go To" player is. The "Go To" is the player you will hit towards if you are facing the two of them at the net or if you don't know exactly where to hit. This is extremely helpful because it relieves you of the pressure that you need to win off your good shots. You win most of your points off of your opponents errors. Find the "Go To" player and dominate like Prem and Clay.

108 Control What You Can

I once heard that there are realistically only two things you can control in life: your effort and your attitude. In tennis, you can control the point to an extent if you hit a great serve or shot, but you cannot control your opponent's anticipation or movement skills. When you are losing and feel like you can't hit well, keep in mind your effort and your attitude. The effort starts with your footwork. Move your feet consistently before the point starts. As for attitude, remember that regardless of the score or the way you feel like you are playing, you are going to be the toughest competitor on the court.

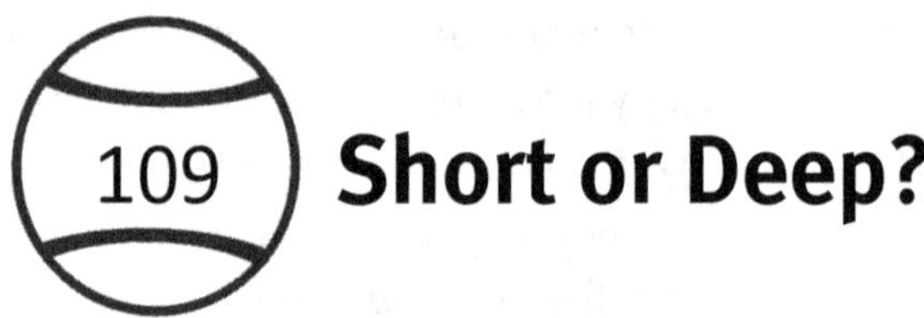

109 Short or Deep?

Do you win more points in doubles hitting the ball short or deep? Oftentime coaches will recommend you hit deep because it is safe and high percentage. When you hit deep, consider where your opponent is. If they are also deep in the court, you are returning the ball directly back to them. On the other hand, if you return the serve at an angle into the service box, you will make the server move from their position and run. This will also set up your partner for a potentially easy volley. What happens when you volley deep? You might run your opponent back, but what if your opponent is strong from the baseline? In this case, you are playing to their strengths. Volleying into the service box forces your opponents to run more and hit up. Whether you return on an angle or volley into the service box, you are eliciting the high response that you want. This gives you a high volley or an overhead and greatly increases your chance to win the point.

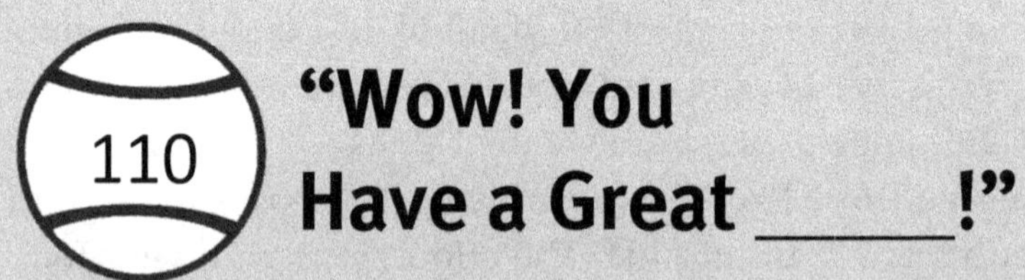

110 "Wow! You Have a Great _____!"

You're playing a match and your opponent has an amazing serve. Their serve is so strong that you and your partner aren't making many returns back. Want to pull a

Jedi mind trick on that opponent? On the next changeover, politely look at the dominating server and say, "Wow! You have a *great* serve!" No matter how they respond, sit down, drink some water, and act like you didn't say a word. Here's what will typically happen next. Your opponent will usually start trying to live up to your compliment by making all of their serves great. However, because they are now overthinking this skill, the serve doesn't live up to their great expectations. When any opponent has a dominating skill, you can politely ask what makes that ability so strong and they will usually try to over impress and make more mistakes in the long run.

111 The Tiger and the T-Bone

You're at the zoo watching the tigers as the trainer comes out to feed them a huge T-Bone steak. When he comes out, the tigers approach him with some serious energy. They can't wait for that T-Bone! In a match, you are up one set and your opponent is serving 30-All, hitting their second serve. If you stand stationary while you wait for the serve, your opponent just needs to focus on executing the serve. Instead of standing, move your feet back and forth in your return position. Move closer to the service line, as if you are the tiger waiting for that T-Bone! Get ready to pounce on your opponent's weak second serve. This movement before the return will make your opponent get tight and there's a great chance they will double fault!

112 The Height of the Shot

If a ball is hit with a high arc will it land short or deep? Unless it's a drop shot, a high ball will usually land deep in the court. If the ball is traveling close to the net, it will likely land short. Being hit closer to the net means the ball will land closer to the ground. If you are at the baseline and you see your opponent's shot traveling close to the net, prepare for a short ball. If the ball is hit close to the net, start moving forward. When at the baseline, if there is a high arcing shot coming towards you, you have two choices. You can step up and take the ball on the rise like my players, Tom and his partner John, or you can step back and lob the high ball, like Steve.

113 One Sets Up the Other

Peggy returned the second serve on a sharp angle and ran the server off of the court. This allowed her partner, Debbie, to put away the next shot at the net. On her next return, Peggy lobbed the net player, then Debbie poached the return. During both points most people would applaud Debbie for putting the ball away. Debbie did close out the points, but to understand *why* Debbie had easy shots at the net is key. It is the one shot that sets up the other shot. When you make your opponents run or hit weak shots, either you or your partner should go after their weak return to close the point. Rather than trying to win points off your initial shot, try to make your opponents struggle then you will have the chance to close out the point. One sets up the other!

114 No Statues for Static Players

When you are at the net and your partner is serving, are you a static or dynamic player? Remember static is stationary and dynamic is dynamite! You want to be dynamic before the returner returns the serve. Get moving even before your partner starts their serving ritual. Your movements distract the returner. This is vital, especially when your partner has a weak serve. Next time you play make it your goal to move before the point starts and be more dynamic like two of my players, Patricia and Brandi. Be so dynamic that the tennis center where you play has to erect a statue in your honor!

115 Watch Your Partner?

When your partner is hitting, you should never turn around completely to look at them. If you turn your body to look at your partner, you risk not being aware of your opponent's position to hit the next shot. Instead, when you are up at the net and the ball is either served out wide or the groundstroke is hit on an angle, you need to see how far off the court your partner is to determine how far you should go towards your partner to cover the middle. Do what Steve and Clint named, the lane change. Turn your head to see where your partner is just like looking in your blind spot while driving to see if the lane next to you is clear. Take a peek at your partner before they hit and make the lane change.

116 Practice with a Purpose

I once watched a video of Roger Federer that executed the ideal way to practice. His hitting partner framed a shot while Roger was up at the net. Roger promptly moved up and smashed the floater. He hit it like it was the game point. After watching a few minutes you could see his focus regardless of what shot he was hitting. To help your own match performance, always practice your fundamentals like you actually are playing in a match. Competition isn't like turning on a light switch. It is a gradual process. You can have fun and banter in between points with your friends, but when the ball is in play, keep your mental game turned on as if you are actually playing a match.

117 The Right Thing is the Right Thing

Have you ever tried to poach but missed? How about hitting an offensive lob that landed a few inches too long? It is natural for you to miss. Never let a mistake deter you from making the same tactical play the next time you are given the same opportunity. You may also make the shot, but your opponent hits an even stronger return. Sometimes your shots don't work out, but understand that one point is just one point. Keep making the right play.

118 Let No One Out Move You

Throughout your tennis career your shots will evolve and improve. Nonetheless, there will be bad days when your shots don't hold up. That is just the way tennis goes. The one aspect of your game that your opponents can't change is your movement. A bad hitting day doesn't mean you have to move poorly. Beginning with your ready position you need to be moving. Move back and forth, or up and back, whichever way that gets your feet going. When you are either the server's partner or the returner's partner, get those feet pumping. Before long, you will get a reputation for having high energy and being someone who chases down every ball. How fast you move doesn't matter, it just matters that you are! Always remind yourself that no one is going to out move you!

119 Never Let Them See You Hurt

You're going to get hit by the ball, especially in doubles. If you play tennis for long enough, it is bound to happen. It is just part of the game. When you do get hit, the most important thing is how you deal with it. A player of mine, KJ, told me that she never wants her opponent to see her in any sort of pain so that they would never have any sort of satisfaction. When you get hit in tennis it's easy to get mad. However, you can't let your anger get in the way of winning the next point. When you show your toughness after you've been hit, you also show your resolve, in that nothing will overcome you during your match. Hang tough and move on!

120 Hidden Miles Per Hour

In tennis, it is always more exciting to hit a fast serve or powerful groundstroke. It just feels good to hit the ball hard. The risk in hitting with power is that you also lose some control. There's nothing wrong with being aggressive, just do it in the correct way. Topspin is how you add hidden miles per hour in tennis. The average player won't track the ball early enough to see the extra topspin on your shots. Loosen up your swings with a closed racket face and swing more vertically to get more topspin. You can be more aggressive with your topspin because the spin pushes the ball into the court without taking your control. Try adding some hidden MPH and spin it to win it!

121 Playing in the Wind

Does the thought of playing in the wind make you cringe? Of all the elements to deal with while playing an outside sport, wind is probably the toughest to deal with. Before you acknowledge the wind to your partner or even worse, your opponents, remember the number one rule about bad conditions: *never* verbalize them. Let you opponents complain first. When they complain, it becomes a real problem they have to deal with. When playing in the wind, there are some tactical adjustments you can make to help your game. Lob more towards the middle to give yourself more space to hit into. When your opponents lob to you, let the lob bounce, rather than taking it out of the air. It's easier to judge the shot after the bounce rather than dealing with the wind. Additionally, get to the net earlier as it is much easier to volley with the wind. When you get to the net first, you force your opponents to have to lob, which is even more difficult on a windy day.

122 Be the Man in the Middle

The height of the net in the middle of the court is exactly 3 feet. Over the alleys, the net is 3 feet and 6 inches. Not only do you have 6 inches of more clearance in the middle, but you have more distance to work with when you hit crosscourt through the middle shot. The majority of shots will be hit either crosscourt or through the middle. Wouldn't you like to control the middle of the court and poach more? You don't have to be a great mover or even a great volleyer. What you want to do is keep an eye on the returner's patterns. Usually on the first point of the match, 30-All, and deuce, they will hit crosscourt. On the game point they will usually play the higher percentage shot through the middle or crosscourt. Take the first opportunity to try to get the ball that is traveling through the middle. Even if you miss, you want to establish to your opponents *you* own the middle of the court. When you cut off the middle you are giving your opponent less space to hit into. Make it your goal to dominate the middle of the court more than your opponents.

123 Drive Middle or Lob

You're at the baseline and the returner came to the net off of your second serve. You are now facing both opponents up at the net. Your instinct is to hit a passing shot and try to win the point. Should you pass them in the alley or hit through the middle? Choose the middle first because you have a lower net clearance. There's a chance neither opponent will hit it because they are confused on who should go for it. If your opponents do return your middle shot, they have fewer angles to hit into from the middle of the court. If you don't feel like you can execute a drive through the middle, hit a lob over the player that has more trouble moving backwards. When you feel pressured by your opponents, just remember to hit one of two high percentage shots, drive through the middle, or lob. Duke and Saban are two smart guys off the courts and execute smart shots in doubles too!

124 Face the Ball

Sometimes a shot will be hit so hard you will get jammed. Being jammed is the feeling of not being able to extend your racket out to the ball. Oftentimes a player's position will be the cause of getting jammed up at the net. For example, your partner is serving to the deuce side and you are up at the net. The returners are playing two-back at the baseline. You poach to the T off the return. The ad player then hits a forehand to your right side and you get jammed. When this happens, I ask the net player to stop and look at their feet. Their feet are usually facing the deuce side player. They volleyed to the T, but didn't move their body to face the ball. Simply looking at the ball does not achieve the same result as completely turning your body and facing the ball. Face the ball so that you can choose either forehand or backhand rather than the ball coming directly at you, leaving your shot jammed.

125 Two Out of Three Times, They Run!

You are in the third set and it's a very close match. Both you and your opponents are getting tired. Time to deliver the knockout punch. You are returning from the deuce side and receiving the second serve. You hit a short and sharp angled shot to run the server off the court. After your partner returns the next serve, I want you to lob your next return over the net player. Lobbing the net player forces the server to run behind the net player. It doesn't matter if you win those two points off of your angled return and your lob. You just made the server run two out of the last three points. Your goal is to make it very difficult for them to hold serve and by running them you are doing just that. This also is a fantastic strategy when you are playing in the heat.

126 Feed Yourself

When working on a shot you are having trouble with or learning a new shot, feed yourself. Bounce the ball to yourself and practice your shot. You don't have to worry about tracking the speed or spin from your opponent's shot. Hit your shot with the purpose of feeling what you want to feel. Remember that tennis is a sport based around timing and rhythm. Once you master the feel of your shot, you can then work on timing the oncoming shot from your opponent. When you are trying to learn how to slice, feeding yourself is very beneficial. Marcia and Laura have developed strong slice backhands because they practiced by feeding themselves.

127 Play Like You Practice

You've probably heard the phrase, "Practice like you play." Many players can tell the difference in their performance in and out of matches. Unfortunately, players feel nervous in matches and tend to overthink their shots. In these situations, I remind players that the ball doesn't know if it is practice or a match. Keep in mind, we are playing recreational tennis. Brad Gilbert once said, "When I am out there playing, I need to win so I can pay for my kids to go to college!" None of us have that same level of pressure when we play. Next time you are in a match, remember how comfortable and relaxed you feel in practice, then play freely and leave the tension for your opponents.

128 Taking Care of Business by Holding Serve!

He was up a set and serving 3-4 but he was a little discouraged. Just a few minutes prior, he and his partner had two break points. They were up a set and a service break would all but close out the match. When they were up, 15-40, the ad player was picturing the rest of his afternoon and how much fun he was going to have after they won. This happens to all players at some point. Assuming they would win one of the next 2 points, then hold serve and be up 5-3, they would win one of the next two games and win the match. Not breaking serve was a mental jolt for the ad player to focus on one thing, holding his serve to make the score 4-4. He knew he couldn't change the missed opportunities to break serve. He instead had a little chat with himself on the change over. "I'm Curt Freaking Schilling! I'm going to take care of my business and hold my serve like a boss! This starts with the first point. Great focus! Total focus! I'm getting the first serve in, right here!" He and his partner held serve at Love, then they broke their opponents. His partner won the next two points on his big serve, lost two, then won two more to close out the match 6-4. After missing out on the break at 3-All, my partner, Chris, and I won 12 of the last 14 points to win 7-5, 6-4. Oftentimes a match can turn within a few minutes. Instead of thinking too far ahead, stay focused in the moment and TAKE CARE OF YOUR BUSINESS!

129 Draw the Line

During your career you will have the great opportunity of making a comeback. You will have bad days and you will also play very worthy opponents. So how do you make a comeback when you are losing? Before you start your comeback, you need to put a stop to what is currently happening. Let's say you are in your car and driving in reverse. Before you can drive forward, you need to put your car in neutral. Coach Bob Pearson, from Berry College, taught us how to apply this concept in our tennis game. Take a few steps behind the baseline and, with your foot, draw a horizontal line. Then, take a deep breath and exhale as you step over that line. Metaphorically, drawing the line is putting the car in neutral and stepping over the line is putting your car in drive. You are putting the bad things in your match behind you and stepping forward to better things. Try it the next time you are losing or in a tough match. I still use this great advice today with my players. Thanks Coach Pearson!

130 Hit Up Like Andre

Back in the 90s, there was a professional tournament in Atlanta called the AT&T Challenge. The mother of one of my students, a wonderful woman named Julia, called me and asked if I wanted to go to the semi-finals with her, her daughter Casey, and Casey's boyfriend Carlos. We sat seven rows behind the baseline! As I watched Andre Agassi warm up, I noticed how he hit upwards so intensely that it looked like his racket was taking flight on his backhand. To this day, whenever I don't have my timing right, I focus on hitting up. By doing this, I get more topspin which is a safer and a higher percentage shot. Eventually your timing improves and you can relax and be more aggressive if you want. The next time your timing is off, hit up like Andre to get some more topspin. When you do this, more balls go in, then you can win!

131 The Golden Rule

The Golden Rule in doubles is to follow the ball. Picture yourself as the ad side player and the serve pulls your partner off of the court. If you stay where you are, there's a big space in the middle of the court between you and your partner. If your opponent ever hits a winner against you, you don't want them to have a big space to hit into.

Stick with the golden rule and follow the ball. When the serve goes wide and your partner goes out to get it, you want to move towards the ball to help you block the middle. It is okay if your opponents hit to a smaller space. However, you don't want your opponent to have a big space, like the middle of the court, as their easy target. In a recent match, Dean was pulled wide off of the court. The opposing net player poached off of Dean's shot. However, Dean's partner Alan moved with Dean and covered the middle of the court. Alan followed the Golden Rule and they won the point!

132 What Time is It?

It's time for you to add spin to your serve! First, use a continental grip. The continental grip allows your racket to impart natural spin on the serve. Secondly, assuming you're right handed, reach up to hit 1 o'clock (top right of the ball). If you're left handed, reach up to hit 11 o'clock (top left of the ball.) When you do this, you will add spin to your serve. This will also allow you to be more aggressive with your serve without losing control. While working on this book I was reminded about this tip by someone that I helped over twenty years ago. Thank you Heather for the reminder, as well as being an amazing mother for our kids!

133 Stop the Ball with a Stop Sign

One of the biggest mistakes made at the net is swinging at the volley. Maybe because your coach told you to *hit* the volley. Hitting usually equates to power when instead you want to have control and touch on your volleys. Being aggressive at the net is easily confused with hitting a hard volley. The volley is just a touch shot. Your movement and activity at the net should be aggressive but your racket movement should be very short on the volley. Hold your hand steady as if your racket is a stop sign.

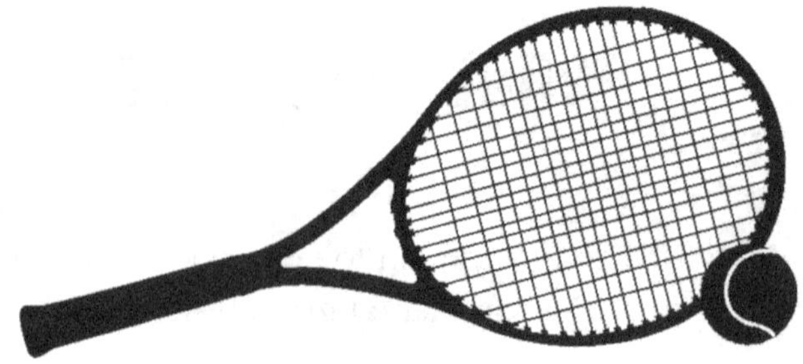

Make It Difficult for Them

Today I witnessed two amazing winners. Marcia hit a great angled forehand and Susan hit a great down-the-line winner. You too will hit some amazing winners. Once you notice which shots your opponents hit well, make it difficult for them to hit the same shot to stop their pattern. You should vary the speed of your next shot to them. Typically, slower shots change their rhythm more. Varying your court position also takes away the opening that they just had. Keep looking for ways to give your opponents different shots and formations to make it difficult for them. Let them have a few winners but don't let them receive the same type shot or see you in the same court position.

Bad Practice? No Worries!

Leaving the court today, Eden said, "I had a really bad practice today!" Last week, Caroline wasn't happy with the way she was hitting during her lesson. I told Eden and Caroline that it's okay to have a bad practice because this can improve your focus in your match. In practice you are getting the repetition that you need to execute your skills in your matches. The work you do in practice builds your preparation and confidence for your match. You are human and you will definitely have bad days, but you can still win even when you aren't hitting as well as you'd like.

136 One Step Back to Move Up Two Levels

Too often when playing the net, players don't move enough. Players will also stand so close to the net that they don't have enough space to move forward. A simple solution is to start one step behind where you want to be. When the point starts and you move forward to where you want to be, you are moving into your volleys. As you learn from experience, the more you move forward on your volleys, the better they are.

137 Easy Makes It Fun

Legendary coach, Jimmy Evert, once said that tennis should be taught in no more than three instructional steps. Coaches often share so much information with players that when they try to remember every little detail they can be overwhelmed. You have an oncoming ball and you don't have much time to reach for it, much less think about the many details of fundamentals. For example, the serve is especially about rhythm: down, up, reach or toss, cut the cake, high five. On groundstrokes you can make your timing easier by simply saying "bounce, hit" when the ball bounces and then you hit. Eventually, you will get to a point where you don't need to think about what you are doing and you just execute your shot to your target. At one point during practice, Honey said, "Wow this is so much fun to do!" Music to a coach's ears!

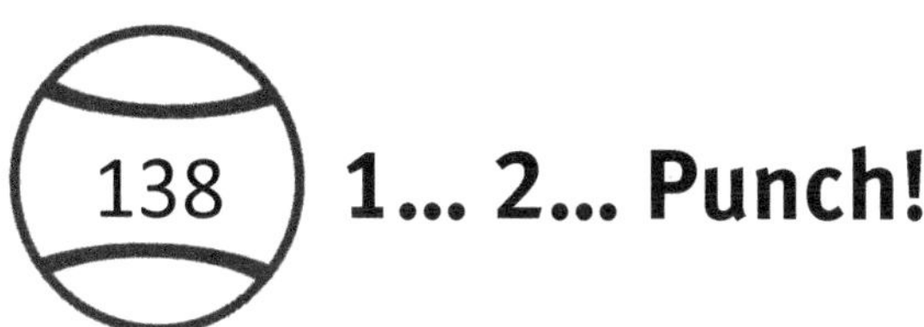

138 1... 2... Punch!

A winning doubles combination or a singles player wins by hitting two shots. The first punch is the shot that puts the opponents in a weak position. The second punch is the shot that wins the point. Lisa has a strong slice forehand, so low, that her opponents have great difficulty returning it. Her forehand slice is punch #1. Lisa's doubles partner, Pam, is very strong at the net. She has great angles, moves well, and has a solid overhead. Pam at the net is punch #2. Their 1-2 punch is Lisa's slice forehand that elicits a weak reply, and then Pam executes a volley winner. Being a good doubles partner is knowing your partner's strength and then capitalizing on your opponent's weak reply. Communicate your strengths to your partner as well so you both can dominate your opponents.

139 A Hammer or a Whip?

Twelve-year-old Sophia was practicing her serve to get more speed and spin. I told her to accelerate her racket. When she tried to accelerate, she did what most people do when they try to produce more power or spin. She actually hit the ball slower. She tightened up her grip and flexed her arm, but was confused as to why she didn't hit with more power and spin. I asked her what would travel faster through the air: a heavy hammer or a whip? She's a quick learner and correctly chose a whip. When you want your racket to accelerate more on groundstrokes or serves you want to loosen up and let your racket head whip. Just think, loosen your grip and let it whip!

140 Bellybutton to the Ball

I say the word "turn" thousands of times per day when teaching groundstrokes. What I won't say, however, is "racket back." Taking the racket back doesn't turn the shoulders or create a unit turn with your body. Too often the shot becomes just an arm action if the player doesn't turn. Your entire upper body is used on groundstrokes, not just your arms. To make a strong unit turn, turn your bellybutton to face the side you are hitting from, whether forehand or backhand. When you rotate your bellybutton your shoulders also turn. Turning this way generates a full body motion that makes groundstrokes fluid and effortless. Turning also helps you hit your coach with the ball, right Tate and Everett?

141 Starting Line, Finishing Line

Do you volley with your hands or with your feet? Hands, right? However, if you don't move your feet and get to the ball, it won't matter how good your hands are. Susan asked how she could close off more points when she volleys. She is a very strong baseliner and has good volleys, but like most natural baseliners, she doesn't continue moving through her volleys. Here's where you can help yourself close out more volleys. Take your normal net position and draw a line with your shoe. That is your starting line. Then, move four feet forward and draw another line. That is your finish line. When the ball comes to you, make your volley and continue moving past your finish line. You will feel great momentum, get to the ball at a higher point, and have more angles to volley into. Crossing your finish line will help you close out more points at the net.

142 Slice = Slow

Whether you are hitting or returning a slice, you must be careful not to swing too fast. If you swing too fast while slicing, the ball can get too much lift and sail out. To prevent this, try slowing down your swing and see how that feels. If you are returning a slice and swing too fast you won't feel very much control as an oncoming slice can stay low and be uncomfortable. You are better off taking a slower swing to get the low ball back in play. Eric is a high school junior and a talented player. I asked him how he should return a low hard slice and he responded, "Hit a neutral ball." Great answer Eric. Hang tough on an oncoming slice and remember to go slowly to keep control.

143 "Why Do I Lose?"

Jenn, a fairly new player, asked this question during a lesson. I answered her with a question of my own, "What happens when you lose?" She explained the many mistakes she and her partner have made that cause them to lose points. The bottom line is that the losing team makes too many errors. Seventy percent of the points lost at the professional level are ended by an error. It is true that they might make tennis look better, but the percentage of errors ending the points is still quite high. You shouldn't focus on winning points, but instead focus on making your shot. Players that try to end the point with winners make too many mistakes. Focus on hitting a high percentage of your shots while trying to make your opponent's shots difficult. Do that, and winning takes care of itself!

144 Take Away Their Time

Read that again. It doesn't say, "Take your time." Take away *their* time! When you run to the ball, especially at the net, you take away reaction time from your opponent. Focus on getting to your volley early rather than trying to hit a powerful volley. When you get to the volley early you also have an easier approach because the ball is higher. The bonus is that your opponent has less time to react to your shot!

145 Say What You Want

Angel has a very strong backhand but feels that her forehand is her weakness. When working to improve a weakness, most players make a natural comparison to their strengths. Forget about trying to make your weakness equally as strong as your best shot. Just focus on making it a reliable shot that your opponent can't exploit. The best way to do this is to say what you want. For example, Angel says, "Lift," to generate topspin in her forehand. Sometimes she will say to herself, "Follow through." Proactive statements like these will help you focus on producing solid, consistent shots, rather than worrying about your results. Say what you want and you will be amazed at how often you can achieve it!

He's Just Like Nadal

One night after practice, I was talking with two players, Mickey and Eric, about Rafael Nadal's perceived weakness. Eric said, "Nadal is just like Mickey… I mean Mickey is just like Nadal." Both Nadal and Mickey have strong forehands. Their backhands might seem like their weaknesses, but they are not weak, just different. Nadal doesn't try to match his backhand to his forehand, rather he plays high percentage backhands and let's his forehand be the punishing shot. If your shot doesn't make errors it is not a weakness, it may just be different. If both your forehand and backhand were the same, your opponents would never have to make adjustments.

147 Sometimes You Have to Go Back at Them

Carson ripped her forehand crosscourt. Her opponent, Robin, returned it crosscourt straight to Carson. On the next point, Jess poached through the middle with a forceful volley towards Kate. All Kate could do was return the ball straight back to Jess. Both returns from Robin and Kate were the correct shots. Carson and Jess hit strong and penetrating shots that were difficult to handle. You would think that you should keep the ball away from the player that just hit a strong shot. However, when receiving a difficult shot, the worst thing you can do is to try to play offense. If a shot is too difficult to change directions, just stay neutral and keep the ball in play. There's a chance your opponents might press too much on the next shot while going for a winner.

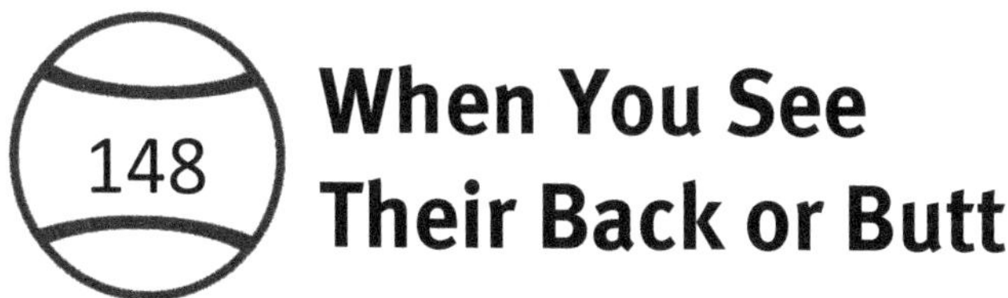

148 When You See Their Back or Butt

Jenny was on the run trying to return the lob that was hit over her partner's head. On the next point, Brandi ran deep in the court to return a high topspin shot. Jenny and Brandi lobbed their shots because they were on defense. When you lob over your opponents, they have to run back to get the lob. When they turn and run, you can see either their back or their butt. As soon as you see either of these, move forward to return their weak shot. When you come in off of your lob, you are turning defense into offense and taking time away from your opponent on their next shot.

149 If It's Hard to Do, It's Good!

A junior player complained about a skill we were practicing, saying, "This is hard to do!" I answered, "Good! It will make you stronger when you accomplish it!" We were practicing hammers, which is the bouncing of the ball off the edge of the racket. One of the six year olds said, "This is too hard!" About thirty seconds later, the same kid yelled, "Yes! I did it!" Do something you don't like or struggle with, like rushing the net or changing your grip to add more spin. A good time to try something difficult is in practice when you are winning 40-Love. If you make a mistake you are still winning. Yes, it might be hard at first but consider the benefits when you learn how!

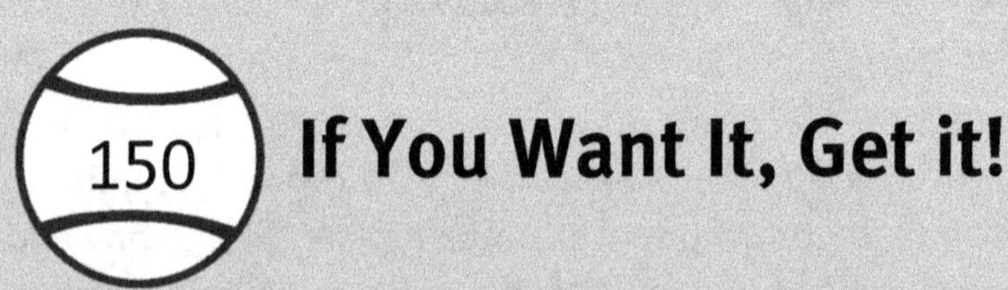

150 If You Want It, Get it!

When should you poach? Poach the ball when you are in the service box moving forward, the ball is above the net, and you have balance. But what if your partner is great from the baseline? Jill and Marjorie were poaching machines today. They asked if they should poach even when they have a good partner. I told them if you want it and you are at the net to go get it! When you poach, you cause many problems for your opponents and greatly increase your chances of winning the point. If you lose the point, don't worry. Your opponents are aware of the threat that you will poach on future points as well.

151 It's More Than a Feeling

Years ago, a racket company had a slogan, "The feeling of a solid shot." Tonight I told two-time Hall of Fame Coach, Rick, that he hit a good shot and he said, "Yeah, but I can't feel it." Rick has great touch and so I believed him when he said he couldn't feel his shot. The good news is that you can win the point even when you don't feel the ball or feel like you are playing well. Some days we don't always feel well but we grind and get on with our lives. The same is true in tennis. You will have those days when you just don't feel your shots and those are the days you just hang in there and grind it out.

152 Find Their Uncomfortable Zone

After a match most players can identify where their opponents like to hit their shots. For instance, one of my players, Art, told me that his ad side opponent did a good job returning low backhands. How often after a match can you identify where your opponents *didn't* like to hit or receive their shots? For example, players with one handed backhands often struggle with high balls. If you can't tell where your opponents struggle, ask your partner what they see. There needs to be a continuous dialog between you and your partner about your opponents struggles. Every player has an uncomfortable zone. They might disguise it well but if you keep looking you will find it and can use it to your benefit.

153 Just Give It a Little Time

Sometimes you need a little longer to warm up and get into the flow of the match. You shouldn't be consumed with your current level of play or even the score. Many things can happen in a short time, so the more patient you are, the better your chance of making a comeback. Remember, it's rare for anyone to be bad for the entire match. It's also rare for someone to be on for the entire match, so just hang tough and give it a little time!

154 Go with Your Momentum

Which direction should you volley when you poach? There's no perfect answer, but the easiest direction to volley is the direction of your momentum. If your momentum is moving towards the right, volley to the right, and vice versa. Then, it's very important to follow your shot. When you follow your shot you will be in line for your opponent's return. Stephanie poached off her opponent's deuce side return. Her volley was to the right of the T. Her opponent was fast and ran it down, only to return it down the middle exactly where Stephanie was positioned. Stephanie won the point because she was in the correct position. Remember to go with your momentum and follow your shot. Good things will happen!

155 Oh, That Was Mature!

Believe it or not, that's not sarcasm. Have you ever been at the net and received a slow, easy ball? Your instincts are to knock the crap out of it and hit a winner, right? Carson is a strong net player and a very good athlete. She received an easy ball at the net and, rather than hitting the ball hard, she lightly tapped it over for a soft winner. One of her teammates yelled, "Oh, that was mature!" Several points later, Brandee did the same thing. A winner is a winner regardless of the speed of the shot. Try being mature the next time you get an easy ball instead of showing aggression. You will drive your opponents crazy!

If You're Going, Keep Going

You move into the court to hit a groundstroke and find yourself in no-man's-land. You could hit your shot then move back behind the baseline, or do what Jim did. After returning a shot in no-man's-land then moving behind the baseline, I told Jim to keep moving forward the next time. Jim moved through his next shot and went to the service line. He reflected that it feels better to keep moving through. Then he added, "If you're going you might as well keep going." You will be naturally moving through your shot and you are also putting pressure on your opponents.

Slight Changes Create Big Rewards

Have you ever played a seemingly endless deuce game? The problem is you and your partner are doing the same things over and over again. Remember the slightest change can reap big rewards. If you are the net player and your partner is serving at deuce, you need to change your position in the service box. When the serve lands in the box, you should move to where you're most comfortable. The fact that you started somewhere else could be the difference in your opponent making or missing their shot. The same applies for the returner. Stand in a different spot and when the server tosses, move to your comfortable spot. You don't necessarily have to change your shots, as the visual of your position change is what makes your opponents overthink.

158 Two Feet Equals Two Levels

Cathy hit an approach shot and the passing shot landed near her feet. Susan returned Leslie's forehand, but had to make an uncomfortable low volley. Both Cathy and Susan are very good players, however, even good players struggle when they have to volley from behind the service line. When you move two feet past the service line the ball you receive will be higher than if you stop at the service line. Not only will you receive a higher ball which is easier to volley, but you gain leverage and angles too. Cathy and Susan are former B-level players moving into the A-level because they moved in just two feet more on their volleys.

159 It's Okay to be Ambidextrous

If you have a two-handed backhand, you know that stretching for a backhand can be a challenge. You could hit a one-handed backhand for more reach, but most players that use a two-handed backhand feel that that is too weak. But what about taking your right hand off the racket and swinging with your left hand? This is actually a left handed forehand but it can work! Several ladies I coach use it often and very well. Just when their opponent thinks they are stretched wide to their backhand, these ladies use a left handed forehand. It's more than okay to be ambidextrous… just ask Margaret, Kathy, Jenn, and Judy!!

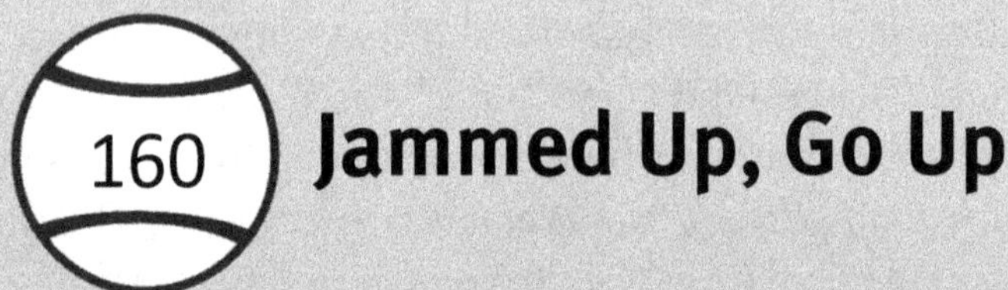

160 Jammed Up, Go Up

Mike is a strong player who can hit big topspin off of his forehand as well as his backhand. He also slices with both sides, too. I showed him how to handle a ball at the baseline that is coming right at him. We have all felt jammed by a ball coming at us because we can't extend to hit either topspin or backspin. It could be a body serve or a strong groundstroke coming right at you. With very little time to react and you feel jammed up, remember to go up. Going up means opening up the racket face to lift the ball up or play a lob. You are on defense so hitting a high percentage shot in this situation is smart!

161 As Often as Possible!

How often should you poach in doubles? If you follow 3 conditions you will poach successfully:

1. Be in the offensive position, inside the service box close to the middle.
2. Contact the ball when it is above net height.
3. Maintain your balance while moving to the ball.

Poach early and often, especially when you feel confident you can make the volley. Let your opponents know that the middle is your area and you will poach as often as possible!

162 You Can't Fix the Last Match

You lost your last match. Fifty percent of all players do! I bet you never thought that half of all players lose. Hall of Fame basketball coach, Bob Knight, said that when he was a kid leaving his house to play any sport his mom would remind him that someone has to lose. Coach Knight would say to himself, "Right, Mom, but it sure as hell doesn't have to be me!" I agree with Coach Knight and so should you. You should believe that you have a strong chance to win in every match you play even though you will lose some. You can't do anything about your losses except to play more matches with the hope to win. Unfortunately, players try too hard to win in their next match as a way to get over the mistakes from the last match. You want to remember where you made errors and make a higher percentage of your shots during your next match. Learn from your tactical and mental mistakes and have the resolve to be better. This is where you grow as a player. Let go of the emotions from your past losses, remember which adjustments to make, and keep playing one point at a time!

163 Scramble and Adapt

My USPTA sponsor and long time mentor, Tom Daglis, was the director of a high performance tennis camp back in the 90s and I was one of his counselors. During one of the strategy sessions, he told the junior players that they only needed to do two things to be great. Scramble and adapt! Of course you need strokes, but much of tennis is defense and if you scramble and adapt you can compete with anyone. My students have definitely heard me say this many times. One of my players, Jess, was forced to play a lot of defense in a recent match. I told her she was doing a great job of playing defense. She looked at me and said, "Scramble and adapt!" Always great to hear your coaching from a student. And thank you for your mentorship, leadership and friendship as well, Tom Daglis!

164 Hitter or Player?

Do you want to be known as a great hitter or a great player? You've seen them before. You walk up to the courts and the player is hitting looking like a pro. Very smooth and technically sound. Their strokes might look good and flashy but during the match their percentages are low. Too often a great hitter who focuses too much on their technique can't adjust to the different shots and speeds during match play. A great player on the other hand, won't be afraid to hit an unorthodox shot or vary their speed to disrupt the rhythm of the hitter. Focus on the competition itself rather than style and people will be talking about how often you win!

165 Keep Them Guessing

Sue is a former softball pitcher that told me she kept the batter off balance with different pitches. Serving is very much like pitching. You want to vary your serves by hitting a slower serve or spinning it more on your first serve rather than consistently hitting a hard serve. Your opponent is also looking for power on your first serve. Your off speed can force mistakes from them. When returning serve, you should also use the same approach. It works to rip the return if you have a serve you can handle and control with pace. Additionally, blocking, chipping, or looping a return can keep the server off balance. Have fun frustrating your opponents with different speeds. Being predictable takes the thought away from your opponents. Do as many things as you can with the ball and watch your win total grow!

166 Put Them in the Corners

In just his fourth lesson, ten-year-old Alex told me his strategy. I had placed a big target in the backhand corner. His objective was to hit toward the target area (Always have a target!). He said, "After I hit to the target, I'm going to hit it to the other side and make him run!" Bingo Alex! A great strategy for singles is to hit to a corner (your target) then hit to the other corner to run your opponent. In doubles, you don't have as much space to run two players, but you can still hit to the sidelines to get one player on the run, then hit the next shot between them.

167 Four Obstacles

High school player Eric was working on his approach shots for doubles. Eric is a singles player, but is learning doubles quickly with his dad as his partner. He is a little apprehensive about approaching the net in doubles because, as a singles player, he's used to having to cover the net by himself. I told Eric about four obstacles the baseliner faces in doubles which made him more confident about approaching the net. The four obstacles the baseliner has to overcome are the net, both opponents, and still keep the passing shot in play. Remember, if you and your partner rush the net and don't cover your alleys, your opponent only has nine feet (4 ½ feet in each alley) to pass you. Keep rushing the net in doubles and make it difficult for your opponents.

168 Try It, You Might Like It!

I prefer to use my two-handed backhand on the return of serve and most groundstrokes. However, I use a one-handed backhand to slice or drop shots, or to chip and charge the net. One of my players, Casey, was trying a two-handed backhand, though he prefers a one-handed backhand. If you have a two-handed backhand, try learning a one-handed, slice backhand. It will likely feel weird, weak, or difficult at first, but give it some time and you will be glad you have another shot you can use, especially on defense. Remember when one of your parents persuaded you to try a food you weren't sure about? Try it, because you might like it!

169 Good Enough

I heard a golfer once say his drive was good enough. He could have hit his shot better, but it definitely could have been worse. Good enough is being content with hitting a neutral or defensive shot rather than being aggressive. You might have a shot in tennis that you can crush. The problem is that if you try to be great, you can often lose control and make an unnecessary error. Even if you do make your great shot, it's still only worth one point. Good enough is really enough to win consistently.

170 Check Yourself

Too often players play based off of their emotions. A player will hit a winner during one point and immediately go for a winner again the next point because of how good they felt after the first. Tennis is *situational*. Each point comes with its own history. Sometimes the ball presents itself as an opportunity for the player to be aggressive and go for a winner. Other times the situation requires defense or a neutral ball from the player. Channel your emotions into your movement and court positioning. Move and attack more often when you are getting fired up. Remember the value of each point is only one, so check yourself and play tennis one point at a time.

171 The Most Bizarre Tennis Injury Ever!

Pulled muscles, torn rotator cuffs, ruptured achilles tendons, and ACL tears. We've all heard of these injuries, but have you ever heard of an overhead causing internal bleeding? Just a couple years ago, Spike was playing his playoff match with Dave. Spike hit an overhead and thought he pulled a stomach muscle. He said the pain was very sharp. They won the match around 9pm, but by 5am the next morning, Spike was at the hospital. I will spare you all the gory details, but he ruptured an artery and had internal bleeding which required emergency surgery. It was touch-and-go for a few hours. After a week in the hospital, he was cleared to go home, and after several months, he returned to the courts. Spike used to dive for balls on the hard courts, not just on clay! He doesn't dive anymore, but his passion for tennis and winning is as great as any player I've ever coached. He gave the idea of leaving it all out on the court a new definition! He definitely earned the award for most bizarre tennis injury ever! If you play tennis long enough, you are bound to have an injury. When you do have an injury, patience is very important. Make sure you are fully healed before you go 100% on the courts.

172 Anxious?

"How do I play when I am anxious?" asked Alex, one of my players. I asked her what she was anxious about. She has only been playing for a couple of years, but all players get anxious. Players get anxious because they want to win! It is totally okay to want to win, but to deal with being anxious you shouldn't focus on winning alone. Winning is a byproduct of you making your shots and your opponents making errors. Sometimes we question our abilities and sometimes we are intimidated by our opponents. Before you think about winning or your opponents, focus on making your shot to an intended target. It doesn't matter at what speed or how much power is on your shot. If your opponent returns your shot, you didn't fail. Isn't your opponent supposed to return your shot? When they return, focus on hitting the ball to your next target. To deal with being anxious, know that you are going to play and compete for two hours. You will have ups and downs because that's the way tennis is. Keep your thoughts simple and forget about the outcome of winning and losing.

173 K.I.S.S.

The question asked was, "How do I win?" My response? Hit to a target and when or if they return it, hit to another target. Sounds simple doesn't it? You've heard that something is simple but not easy? Think of the acronym: K.I.S.S. Keep It Simple and Straightforward. That's how you should play. Hit to your target and expect the ball to come back. When it does, hit towards another target or even the same target. You shouldn't think about winning so broadly because many things are out of your control. What *is* in your control are your thoughts about where you are hitting your shots. Keep it Simple and Straightforward!

174 DEFENSE!

"It's a good thing I have defense," Renae said during practice. Renae has plenty of offense too, but she plays great defense. When she has a difficult shot she always makes sure to hit a soft shot to maintain control. Nicole is a former softball and track star. When she runs down difficult shots that are seemingly out of reach, she plays defensively with lobs or slower groundstrokes. Like Renae and Nicole, you might be talented and athletic, but it can help your game to learn to play defense. Practice hitting slower on all of your shots. You will gain control when you hit slower which keeps the ball in play!

175 50%, 75%, But Not 100%

No, these weren't my math scores in high school! B.A. has a backhand that looks like a baseball player hitting a home run. Hake and Pork Chop hit booming overheads. These men have powerful shots but they don't use 100% of their power. They understand that hitting as hard as you can is low percentage tennis. Low percentage is also the recipe for losing! Hitting with 50% or 75% of your power will still get the job done. You are applying pressure to your opponents while playing at a high percentage. Your recipe for winning is making a high percentage of your shots while forcing errors from your opponents.

176 Outside = Angles

How does it feel to hit a solid shot? It feels like you're hitting the ball smack in the middle. Isn't that what you're supposed to do? Becky and Michelle were working on hitting groundstroke angles away from the net player and trying to run the server with their angles. Unfortunately, when they hit the middle of the ball, their shots went down-the-line or through the middle of the court. The middle of the court is too close to the opposing net player. I told Becky and Michelle to hit the outside of the ball. Hitting the ball on the outside creates angles on your groundstrokes. To practice this skill, try this. Bounce the ball in front of you and try hitting the outside of the ball. After you develop the feel of getting more angles, hit some shots from your hitting partner. You will soon realize that the outside = angles.

177 You Get What You Say

Suzie was a poaching machine this morning. One of her teammates said, "We have to keep the ball away from Suzie." Unfortunately they hit more balls near Suzie because they were thinking about Suzie. A better way to think is by saying, "Let's hit to the opposite side of the net strap." When you focus on what you don't want, you actually do that very thing. Instead, picture exactly what you *do* want. You can visualize it to yourself or speak it out loud; it doesn't matter. Just focus on what you do want to happen. You get what you say!

178 Spin It to Win It

Many players like hitting the ball hard. They assume that if they hit the ball hard, their opponent will make a mistake. In reality, if you hit hard and don't add topspin you will make a lot of mistakes and lose! During a practice, I was working with Tyler, a former baseball player in his early 40s. He was hitting strong groundstrokes that were line drives, much like hitting a baseball. At one point, another player, Carter, was hitting tentatively. I told him to rip upwards on the ball to generate more topspin. When both Tyler and Carter saw how many more shots went in with topspin, they both had more confidence. It's okay to be aggressive and want to hit hard, but make sure you hit up on the ball to generate more topspin. See how much topspin you can add to make the ball feel very heavy to your opponents.

179 Hit Their Hat

During their warm up drill, KJ and Susan were hitting the net frequently. When we switched sides Leslie and Kathy were hitting the net frequently as well. This had nothing to do with the skills of these four women. Have you ever noticed that you miss frequently as you are warming up? Give yourself a break! You haven't warmed up enough! Often it's not a stroke mistake but more of your aim or target. Aim for where your opponent's hat would sit while they are up at the net in warm ups. Their hat is usually around two feet above the net height. Keep your focus above the net and you won't be making the worst mistake in tennis!

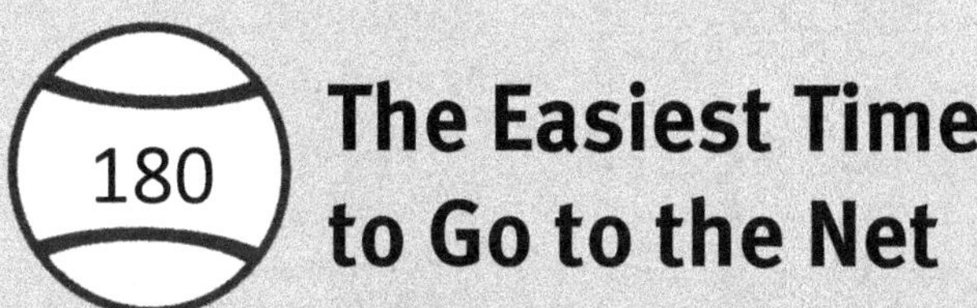

180 The Easiest Time to Go to the Net

Players will often ask when is the best and easiest time to approach the net? If you are at the baseline and your partner receives an easy ball, all you have to do is get to the service line before your opponent hits. You don't have to hit an approach shot or worry about its strength. All you have to do is move in when your partner plays their easy shot. Your opponents will most likely hit a weak reply off of your partner's shot and you don't want to have to scramble to get there when you have control of the point. Move in and take away space from your opponent's weak return.

181 Move Better

I always enjoy learning from tennis players that excel in other sports. Ten year old Rohan is a top swimmer. He's been playing tennis for about a year. Like many juniors, he sometimes gets flat footed waiting for the ball. I asked him to show me how a swimmer starts on the starting block. He showed me and I asked him why he was on the balls of his feet and not on his heels. His response was, "Because you go faster!" You will move better on the court as well if you get on the balls of your feet. Before the point starts you should get your feet moving. One of the best ways to get on the balls of your feet is to remember to hop or bounce when the ball bounces on your opponent's side of the court. Bounce on the bounce and see how quick you can be!

182 Too Early to Judge

Ever have a bad warm up? Does that guarantee you're going to have a bad day and lose? You can never know for sure. Some days you just need time to warm up and you will be fine after a few points into the first set. If your opponent has a bad warm up or misses a few shots early *do not* assume you will win! If they are missing, that is great.

Keep doing what you are doing and continue to force errors, give them different looks, and apply anything else you can to make the match difficult for them. You want them to question everything they are doing because you and your partner never let up. There's nothing worse than losing a match because you misjudged your opponents by a few early mistakes. Put it in your head that it's a two hour battle, and you and your partner won't let up until you win!

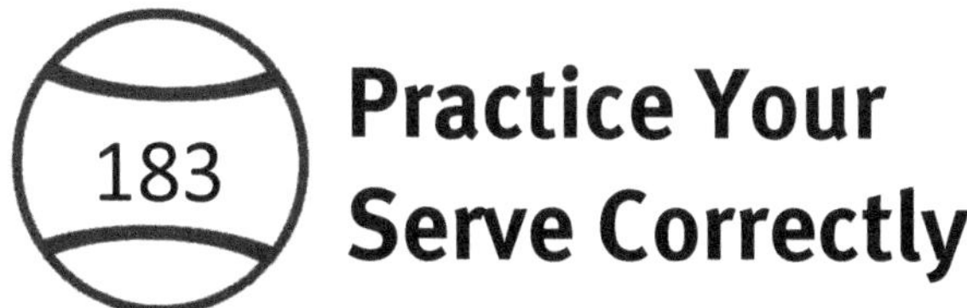

183 Practice Your Serve Correctly

I love seeing a player with a basket of balls practicing their serve. This shows me that the player cares about winning. You want to be sure that when you go up to the baseline, you have a reliable serve. Typically, most players hit about fifty balls to the deuce side, then several more to the ad side, and then call it a day. Here is a better way to practice your serve so that come match time, your serve will be an asset for you. First, you should practice your second serve. After your second serve is warmed up, grab two balls. Put one in your pocket like you do when you play. Go ahead and serve like you would in a match. When you make your first serve, take the other ball out of your pocket, toss it a few feet in front of you, and hit a groundstroke. This simulates your opponent returning your serve and you playing the point. If you miss your first serve, hit your second serve. Then do the same on the ad side. Go back and forth from deuce to ad like you are playing a match. Former top 10 world ranked player, Tom Gorman, told me that after hitting several serves he would sprint to the net and back to get his heart rate up. This is also a great way to simulate the feeling of playing a rally after you serve as well as getting into better shape. Remember to practice your serve like you are playing a match, so when you are actually playing a match, it feels comfortable rather than stressful.

184 It's Okay to Be Different

What is your strongest shot? What is your weakest shot? Typically, players prefer their forehands over their backhands, yet several of my students like to use backhands more often. A common mistake is trying to make your weakest shot just as powerful as your strongest shot. For instance, if you have a strong topspin forehand and an average topspin backhand, you may want to improve your backhand, but you should realize that it might never be as strong as your forehand. Rather than trying to make your weakness as powerful as your strength, work on your consistency and make your weakness a reliable shot. If you aren't making errors off your weaker shot, then it actually is a good shot. Remember, the contrast between your strength and the weaker, but reliable shot still affects your opponents.

Because It's Tennis!

"Why do we have to run and hit?" asked Tate and Everett. Because it's tennis! I often alert students when I feed them a challenge ball. A challenge ball is a ball hit away from the player to make them run. Soon after learning the basic fundamentals, you need to practice hitting on the run. Think about what your opponent is trying to do. Would they want to hit the ball directly to you or try to make you run? When you have to run for a groundstroke, turn immediately and then move. Getting your racket prepared early with a shoulder turn will help you make your shot once you arrive at the ball. There should be zero panic about winning or losing the point. Your job is to get to the ball and make your opponent have to hit at least one more shot if they are going to win the point.

Never Smell Like Should

Whenever you have hesitancy about doing something, you should still do it! If you try but lose, at least you still tried. Being afraid to try leaves you wondering what might have happened. Your actions smelling like "should" makes losing even worse! The next time you think about doing something different, do it! Never smell like should! Remember it's more fun to have courage and be bold!

187 Talk Yourself Up!

If you've recently been doing something counterproductive on the court, you have the ability to change the bad habit. Jenn had been stopping her forehand before completing her follow through. I gave her some corrections and for the rest of the hour she hit without a problem. One week later, I asked her how her forehand was. She said that before she hits her forehand she tells herself to follow through. Another player, Christy, was working on getting more angles on her groundstrokes. I told her to focus on hitting the outside of the ball and to say "outside" before she hit. She did this and her groundstrokes improved throughout the rest of the practice. Your brain will help you achieve what you say rather than what you want to prevent. Talking yourself up isn't a pep talk but instead it helps you focus on what you want and with your execution of your shots.

188 DEFEND

You are inside the service box and your opponent lobs to you. What is your first instinct? Do you let your partner get it or are you determined that no ball will get over your head and then turn to reach their lob? If your instinct is to switch, you are automatically on the defensive. Your partner has to run deep into the court and handle a high bouncing ball. If you can turn to block the ball out of the air, you and your partner have the advantage. The mistake comes when you think that you have to hit a strong overhead. If you are moving backwards, you shouldn't be aggressive. You should just block their lob back in play to defend your court position. Have the mindset that you will defend their lob before you choose to switch.

189 Easy Balls Make You Lazy

It's natural that when you have an easy shot, you relax. Many players make the mistake of losing their focus because they think the point is guaranteed. Oftentimes, players stop moving when they see the oncoming easy ball. Eighty percent of all errors are footwork related. The next easy ball you receive, exaggerate one good fundamental. Focus on moving more, keeping your head still, or hitting a specific part of the ball. Remember to focus on executing your shot, rather than assuming you have already won the point.

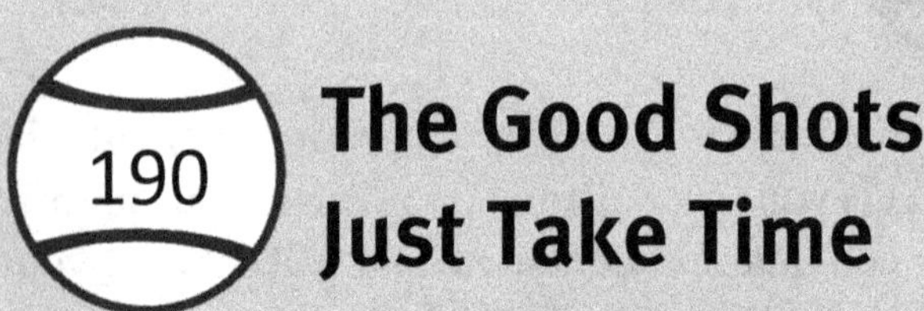

190 The Good Shots Just Take Time

Do you know much about wine? I personally don't, but I've heard something along the lines of, "Fine wine takes time." Before you go grab a glass, think about your progressions as a tennis player. For instance, to hit a good slice serve, you need to use the continental grip. You could just push the serve in with an Eastern grip, but your serve will always be average. It takes many good repetitions to learn and feel the continental grip and develop a good spin serve. How about your drop shot? How many times have you hit a bad drop shot before it became a weapon? Part of the fun of becoming a good tennis player is going through the struggles and then seeing your time and effort pay off.

191 More Win!

"More Win" was a slogan used several years ago by Wilson. Of course your goal is to win but to win you need to add to that slogan. More in means more win! There will be a match in your future when you aren't playing well, or you are hitting well but losing. Keep things simple and tell yourself to start with "more in," then go from there. Get a higher number of balls in play to put more pressure on your opponents. Winning will take care of itself if your percentages are high. Your high percentage also forces errors from your opponents. Remember: more in = more win!

192 The Great Ones Slow It Down

Usually when people think about this statement, they think the great ones slow their shots down, when they actually slow things down before the point even begins. Rather than thinking about what they can't control, they take deep breaths through their nose and exhale out of their mouths. Go ahead and do that now, four or five times. Before the point starts, take a few deep breaths, move back and forth, spin the racket in your hand to keep your hands relaxed, and then look across the net. Keep a loose grip until just before contact. Now keep your focus on tracking the ball. You want to keep everything simple before the point begins.

193 Under the Belly Button, Over the Belly Button

We've all done it. You hit a great groundstroke and it feels strong and solid, until it hits the tape and falls back onto your side of the net. When this happens, players will ask, "That felt so good; what went wrong?" When you hit straight it's important to recognize gravity and realize that the ball isn't traveling straight, it's actually moving downward. So what did you do wrong? Your swing pattern is linear. Before you hit, make sure your racket head is under your belly button and then when you follow through, bring your elbow above your belly button. Have a target several feet above the net so your shot is guaranteed to clear it.

194 Interrupt Them!

Have you ever been right in the middle of speaking an important sentence and someone interrupts you? It doesn't feel great. The next time you are up at the net and you see a ball that you could poach, I want you to think about interrupting your opponent. Your opponent is hoping to hit a safe crosscourt shot away from you but how do you think they will feel if you step forward and poach their shot? You are interrupting their rally.

Too many players back off from poaching because they think they won't win the point with their volley. You don't have to win with your first volley, but by poaching, your opponents have less time and will likely hit a weaker shot back to you. Keep interrupting them and they will start to make even more mistakes.

195 There Are No Points for Style

During difficult situations, you play in survival or even panic mode. Players often ask what their technical mistake was when they miss a shot. Keep in mind that there's a difference between making an unforced error versus a forced error. When you are on defense, you should do whatever you can to get the ball back in play. If you do lose any of these points, it is a forced error because your opponent hit a good shot. Players too often think they have to have perfect form or proper technique. In difficult situations there are no points for proper technique or style so do what you can to get the ball back in play and continue to grind!

196 It's Always In

You're at the baseline and your opponent hits a very deep shot. It is also high in the air and you think it's going out. It then lands and it's in! You didn't return it because you thought it was going out. Your first mistake was assuming the ball was going out. You should expect every shot to go in, until it lands. One of the most common mistakes I see is when a player stands a foot inside the baseline and they play the deep ball out of the air. They're not sure if it will land in or out so they play it regardless. If you stand behind the baseline, you can let the ball bounce and know if it's in or out. Always assume your opponent's shot is landing in and be ready to play every shot.

197 Gorilla Slam!

You're up at the net and your partner drives your opponent deep behind the baseline. They return a weak shot. Not only is it weak, but it is floating high and looks like a big beach ball approaching you. It's time for you to hit your huge gorilla slam! What do you do if you don't receive an easy overhead? Former Assistant Coach for the Berry College women's team, Beth Gorman, told me to never hit the first overhead hard. If you are set up with an easy overhead and you hit it past the service line, it will be penetrating and difficult for your opponents to return. If they do return your first overhead, it will most likely be a very weak return then you can be more aggressive with the second overhead. You don't have to hit a gorilla slam to be effective but if you have an easy one go ahead and BOOM!

198 Swing Like You Know It's Going In

If you question whether a shot will go in or not, you will most likely miss. When you question your shot, your body gets tight and you slow down your swing, which results in a very average shot. It has very little spin and your opponent will have an easy ball. If you were up 40-Love, would you approach your shot or serve the same way? With this score, you would probably be more relaxed and swing with confidence. When you hit a topspin groundstroke or a spin serve, you want to be as loose as you can and swing freely. My challenge to you is to forget about the score and the consequences if you miss. You want to hit like you know the ball will go in and swing freely. This will help you add spin to your shots and play the way you intend to.

199 The Heat and the Heavy

Your forehand is your big shot, but you want your backhand to be just as strong. Unfortunately, it probably won't ever be the weapon your forehand is. My college doubles partner, Tony Wright, once said, "I can't figure it out. My backhand was on today and yesterday my forehand was on." Like what Tony describes, you will very rarely find a day that both shots are "on." Try to remember this. You have the heat and the heavy. Your heat is the aggressive groundstroke that is on and the heavy is the other groundstroke that isn't on, but because you are hitting with topspin it is the heavy. The heavy is high-percentage and rarely misses. You can go after the winners with your heat.

200 Touch for Touch

How great would it be to place all your volleys exactly where you want them to land? To hit accurate volleys, you need touch on the ball to control your placement. A common mistake with volleys is to hit with power. If you place the volley to your intended target the speed doesn't matter and it will help your accuracy. Touch the ball to get more touch.

201 New Balls

"Are these new balls?" The answer to two-time Hall of Famer, Ricky Vaughan, was no. Mike and Tom also agreed that the balls must have been new as many of the balls were flying out. Paulette set the men straight and said, "They were new last week; tonight it's just the heat." She was correct. Tennis balls travel faster in warmer air. There are less molecules in warmer air which allows for the balls to move faster and more freely. Colder air has more molecules, which makes it feel like the balls are moving slower in the cold. When temperatures are higher, you should compensate by adding more spin to keep the ball in, as well as having a bigger target giving you more space to hit into.

202 Nell Carver

On Super Bowl Sunday in 1983, I was taking a serving lesson from Hall of Fame Coach Nell Carver. Nell began with my toss, saying, "That's good but slow down." When my toss was controlled, she worked on the rest of my serve. "Slow down, even slower." I slowed everything down and after twenty more she said, "Even slower." Over and over again at a snail's pace. After about 60 serves, I realized my toss was in the same spot and I felt the sweet spot on my racket at contact. She said, "When you practice this, I want you to hit fifty at the same speed before you even think about hitting the ball hard." To this day I have a strong serve and I owe it to Nell for helping me find my rhythm. Anytime I have needed to get my groove back, I remember Nell's advice. Nell was an amazing pro, director of tennis, builder of tennis programs, and had relentless energy. We played a couple of mixed doubles tournaments together and people thought we were a mother/son team. If you were lucky enough to have known Nell you would always remember her encouraging words, her sweet southern voice, and amazing smile. Love you Nell, rest in peace!

203 If It's There, Pull the Trigger

Talking to Prem about closing out the point, recently, he brought up something all players think about. He asked about going for your shots even if it's game point. The common mistake in matches is thinking too much about the score. Regardless of who is ahead, you need to play the shot that is given to you. If you are losing you should play more higher-percentage shots. You can be a little more bold if you are winning. The last thing you should ever do is play tentatively because you are afraid to lose. If you have the chance to go for a winner, go for it! You want tunnel vision to your target and the belief that you *will* make your shot. If it's there, pull the trigger and commit to your target.

204 Get a Head Start

Do you move as quickly as you did in your 20s? Me neither! It's natural to lose a step or two as you get older. Your reactions might be a little slower, but one way to give yourself more reaction time is to start at the service line instead of inside the service box while your partner is serving. But shouldn't you be in the service box so you can poach and gain leverage and angles? Yes, you should, but when you start at the service line, you give yourself a head start. When your partner serves and the ball lands in the service box, start moving forward. You should take one or two steps then split step to get ready to pounce or poach on the return. By getting a head start you will feel more proactive because you are moving forward, rather than waiting to move after the return. Vary your position in the service box and see where you feel most comfortable. As a bonus, your movement distracts the returner and prevents them from focusing on the return.

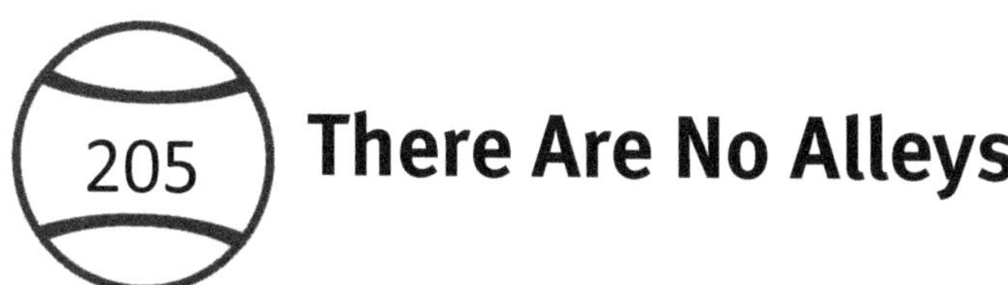

205 There Are No Alleys

The alleys are four and a half feet wide. That's not much space to work with when returning a serve from deep in the court. When players try to hit an angle into the alley they often miss wide. A helpful visual is to ignore the alleys and try to keep your return in the singles court. You can aim just inside the singles sideline and still hit a good angle. When you try to keep your return inside the singles court and miss, you have the benefit of using the alley as a cushion. You should use the same strategy when volleying. Hitting an angle runs your opponent so even if they do reach your shot, they will be hitting a weak shot back to you.

Close the Shower Curtain

The high volley is a shot that looks easy but is often missed down into the net or several feet long. It's not high enough to be attacked like an overhead, though it is very close. Missing beyond the baseline and in the net is the result of swinging. If you picture yourself closing a shower curtain your arm moves forward several feet. That's what you should visualize as you are making your high volley. It's okay if your high volley is not a winner because you end your swing in an offensive position with a good chance of receiving another easy ball from your opponent.

207 The Tidal Wave

You and your partner have decided to play two-back at the baseline returning serve. You would play two-back because your opponents have strong serves, they are poaching effectively, or you just want to give the serving team a different look. Your opponent misses the first serve and has a weak second serve, so now you and your partner are on the offensive. When you or your partner return the second serve, you should both rush into net position. This is what I call the tidal wave. The server and server's partner feel like a tidal wave is approaching them. There's not much space for them to hit into and because they see two people charging at them, they usually panic and rush their shot. They will likely miss right away and you don't have to volley. If you happen to lose the point, keep coming in together and apply pressure. They will make many mistakes because of the pressure of the tidal wave constantly approaching them.

208 Lob Over My Head

How is that a good strategy? It's not a strategy but rather it is a mindset. Two of my players, Brandi and Elke, are not tall and they seem like easy targets to lob over. It doesn't matter how tall you are, if your opponent receives an easy ball and they have a good lob, their potential to lob over you is much greater. Here's your solution to the dreaded lob over your head. Start farther back in the service box or even at the service line. When you do this you are taking away space behind you where their lob could land. You should also pick up on their body cues like leaning back or opening the racket face because that indicates that they are about to lob. As soon as you see the lob go up, turn immediately. Covering just one or two of their lobs can deter them from lobbing you throughout the match.

209 It's Because of the First Shot

If you asked the average person which shot won the point they would usually say the last one. Of course the last shot ends the point. What is important to understand is how and why the player had an easy last shot to win the point. During a recent lesson, Sarah was putting shots away continually. When I asked the other three ladies why Sarah was putting away easy balls, Pat said, "It's because of the first shot." The first shot forced a weak reply by the opponent then Sarah was able to finish the point. Regardless if you won or lost a point, try to remember the shot that set up the finishing shot. If you're winning, keep that pattern going. If you are losing, you can recognize their pattern and give them different shots that won't set them up.

210 Sit on the Slice

When trying to return a sliced ball hit towards you, sit on the slice. Sitting on the slice is just like when you sit down. You drop down with your legs and your butt like you are sitting down. Master pro, Ken Dehart, explains this concept as, "Dropping into your drive." I often phrase this as, "Sitting into your hit." A good fundamental on all groundstrokes is bending with your knees. Don't get caught up in deciding which knee to bend, simply drop your butt like you are sitting in a chair. This will allow you to get under the ball when you hit your slice. You can also use this when a ball is sliced towards you. In these situations, sit to get under the ball so you can lift it back into play.

211 The T is the Bullseye

Your partner hits a great serve which forces a very weak return from your opponent. The easy ball you have been dreaming about is heading your way. It's high, traveling slowly, and you know you can put it away with a volley. It's as if you have an ocean of space to hit into. Your target for most of your volleys should be the T on the court. Aiming for the T helps you hit between your opponents with plenty of court space. Think about the T being the bullseye. There's plenty of space around the T in case you miss it directly. Usually when players miss, their target is too small. Aiming for the T gives you a big target and court space.

When You See Them Drool

You are up at the net and your partner hits a very short lob. You know your opponent is going to slam it based on the way he turns and moves forward. Unfortunately your partner didn't give you any warning that the lob was short. Your opponent is practically drooling as he's winding up to hit his overhead. As soon as you read that he's aggressively moving forward, you should move back. You will gain precious milliseconds of reaction time and set yourself up with a chance to block the overhead and put it back in play.

Neutralize the Net Team

You receive a ball at the baseline and the opposing team moves forward so both players are up at the net. Your instinct is to go for a passing shot towards the closest opening you can see. If you received the shot near the alley, you might be tempted to hit into the same alley in front of you. The alley is only 4 ½ feet wide, so there's limited space to hit into. Also understand that if the net person volleys your shot, they have plenty of angles to hit into. Instead of hitting into the alley, try hitting a higher percentage shot down the middle of the court. There's a chance that your opponents won't know who should play the shot between them. If someone does play your shot, they have less angles through the center of the court. You will also have a second opportunity to force an error from them, should they make their first volley.

214 Two Sneaky Shots

I call these sneaky shots because they can surprise your opposing net player. As a right handed player, if you're on the deuce side and the ball comes down the middle towards your backhand, the most logical shot would be to hit crosscourt. This is a good opportunity for the opposing net player to cut across the middle and poach your shot. Knowing that most net players are looking to poach, now is a good time to drive your shot down-the-line or even directly at the net player. This works especially well coming off of a second serve that pulls you into the court. The second sneaky shot is on the ad side. On the ad side you can run around your backhand and hit your forehand down-the-line. Being inside the court as well as returning the weaker second serve increases your chances of forcing an error from the net player. If you can hit these two sneaky shots at the weaker of your two opponents, you will win even more points. If you're left handed, a forehand on the deuce side and backhand on the ad side will do the same damage.

215 Wilson Tattoo

Have you ever been hit with a volley or overhead? This is what I call a Wilson Tattoo. It's inevitable if you play tennis long enough that you will be hit by a ball. This is especially true if you are playing doubles. Getting hit or even hitting someone with the ball is totally legal and just part of the game. There will inevitably be some tension when someone gets hit by the ball. After you hit someone, remember this. My long time friend and the Director of Tennis at Dunwoody Country Club, Dave Dvorak, gave this advice at a seminar: When you hit someone with a ball, look at them and say, "I'm sorry if I hurt you." You don't have to overreact if they are mad. Just tell them you're sorry if you hurt them. Remember the pain of getting hit by a tennis ball is temporary and the pain of losing the point hurts worse!

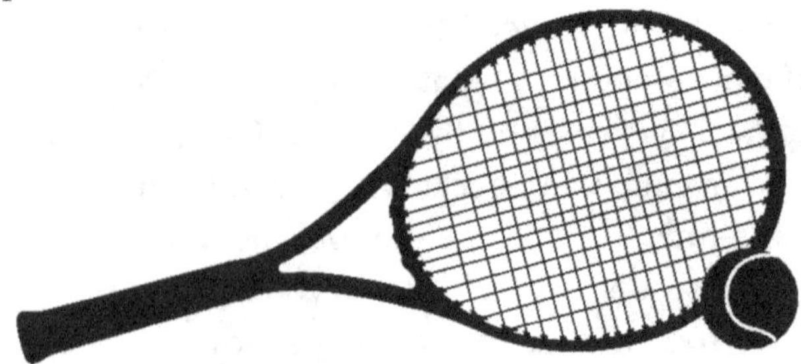

216 Like Your Middle Name Is Fearless!

Tennis is a recreational sport. It is just a game even though your goal is to win. Winning is the main objective. There are much more substantial losses in life than the end of a tennis match. Though I do understand the feeling of losing is terrible. Picture yourself serving 4-5, ad out, and hitting the second serve. Do you believe you're going to make that second serve or afraid that you will double fault? Or are you willing to be bold and poach when your opponent returns down the middle within your reach? How will you feel ten minutes after the match? How about a week later or a month later? Do you want to look back on your match and remember being tentative or being bold? Be bold! Your middle name is fearless! You can even tell yourself before your match, "Today I'm going to be bold. Today I am going to be fearless. Today I am going to be relentless!" You've got nothing to lose even if the match doesn't end in your favor.

217 What Is Your Athletic Background?

I always ask new students if they played any sports growing up. I also like to find out who has played an instrument. Players can easily relate the fundamentals of tennis to other sports or activities they have been a part of. We as instructors can also learn from what the student tells us about their other experiences. For instance, my player, Jenn, told me about her experiences with the baton. Just like any sport, skill or instrument, there's a learning curve. The gratification comes from seeing your skill level improve and what progress is made because of your repetition, dedication and sacrifice. When I was in fifth grade, my love was basketball. Westminster College coach, Ron Galbreath, put his hand on my shoulder one day and said "Carv, you're getting better. Just remember, you can never be too good!" As you progress in your tennis career you will have some days that you feel like you've mastered the sport or know everything you need to know. Keep an open mind, stay curious, and continually grow!

218 You Don't Always Poach the Return

Part of the fun and satisfaction of coaching is when your player or student shares their wisdom. My player, Mike, and I were talking about poaching and he said, "You don't always poach the return." What Mike was referring to is that you can poach other shots during a point and not just the return. Too often, players think that you should only poach off of the return of serve. Sometimes, the return is close to you, but was hit too hard or too low for you to make an effective volley. In those situations it is best to let your partner at the baseline take the shot because they have more time to do so. Then after your partner returns the shot, you should keep looking for your chance to poach. Make it your goal to be the first player to make the first volley. Usually the first team to volley will win the point because you make your opponents scramble to get to your volley.

219 Right Now!

During lessons most players engage better when we keep score. Pam is a strong player and when she and her partner are losing she often says, "Ok, right now!" What she is saying to her partner is to forget about the last point and move on, right now. It doesn't matter how they lost the last point or what the score is but she says this consistently during lessons and her matches. This is a great mindset to have especially when you are losing. You can't change the previous points but you shouldn't think too far ahead. What your focus should be all about is, "Right here, right now!" Keep your focus one point at a time.

220 Slow n' Go

Serving is all about rhythm. There are many moving parts to the serve and trying to focus on all of them at once can make the serve feel stiff or rigid. Your thoughts should be about *where* you want to hit the serve, rather than thinking about how to execute the serve. It is okay to tell yourself something proactive, such as, "Top of the ball," or, "Head up." Avoid making the mistake of giving yourself several directions at once. Whenever you are working on your serve, a great way to improve your rhythm is to start slow, then go. The slow speed at the beginning helps you get a reliable and consistent toss. "Go" refers to the uncoiling of your body as you swing. Try saying this phrase as you practice to hone your focus on these two steps.

221 Find Their Struggle

You hit a high, loopy approach shot to your opponent's backhand and they miss it! For the next approach, you drive it to their backhand again and they hit a passing shot. You drive the next ball and approach their backhand again, but then they hit a good lob. You and your partner decide your opponent has a good backhand and are hesitant to attack again. This is a common mistake that can be avoided. Players tend to remember the good things our opponents do and forget where they struggle. Your opponent might have a good backhand when they receive a drive, but missed your high, loopy backhand. Even if they make a few shots, you can tell when they are hitting if they are comfortable or struggling. Keep discussing these weaknesses with your partner throughout the match so you can find their struggle!

222 See Your Wristband

If you learned how to play tennis from the baseline you might have trouble with your volleys because of the different shoulder movements. When you hit groundstrokes, you turn your shoulders to make a unit turn and complete your swing. If you are more comfortable with groundstrokes, you might struggle with your volleys because you turn your shoulders before you volley. When you turn your shoulders, your racket goes backwards which makes it more likely that you will volley too close to your body. You want to make your contact out in front of your body as if you are catching a ball. In the ready position at the net, if you look down you will see your hands in front of you with your wristband in front of your body. You should see your wristband in front of you as you make your contact in front of your body.

223 The Paralysis of Analysis

You move into no-man's-land to return the short ball. You then stop and watch your shot to see where it lands and where your opponent will hit the shot. They returned it right to you and because you are in no-man's-land, you're unsure if you should bounce or volley it. This can also occur when you hit a strong groundstroke. You hit, stop, and watch only to see your opponent block it back short, and now you are on the defensive. This is what I call the paralysis of analysis. *Always* believe that your opponent will return your shot. After making your shot, either get into the service box or behind the baseline. When you commit to moving in on offense or going back behind the baseline on defense, your options for your next shot become very clear.

I Always Miss My Overhead

When my player, Christie, said this, it was immediately after she had just made three out of her last five overheads! What she was really saying was that she didn't hit enough winners with her overhead. Realize that when you hit an overhead that your opponent is on the defensive. They might have tried to hit an offensive lob but it wasn't deep enough to get over your head. The mistake players make is getting too tense before they hit the overhead. When you are relaxed you get a loose swing which will help generate power. Even more important than power, is hitting the overhead past the service line deep into the court.

225 Push Your Pinky

I love when players intentionally slice. A sliced groundstroke causes many problems for opponents who like pace and a waist-high ball. During their practice, Lauren and Chrissie were using their slice on offense and defense. When I mentioned to Lauren that her slice was very good, she said she really didn't know how to slice! I told her to keep pushing her pinky forward as she hit. Too often players break their wrist and try to cut the ball to create a slice. To practice a correct slice, bounce a ball in front of you and push your pinky forward as you move your racket through the shot. Use the slice and see how you can frustrate a player who hits hard.

226 You're Fine at the Line

You've received a short ball and you return it and move it's position. You are now close to the service box, but are afraid of two things. You don't volley well and your opponent has a good lob. If you stop before you get to the service line, you will have a very difficult volley. If you move in too far in the box, your opponent has plenty of space to lob over your head. The best way to cover the lob and make the volley is to stop at the service line. The service line is three feet closer to the baseline, so you will have time to turn and cover their lob. When you volley you are moving forward so you will be inside the box as you make contact. Next time you move in on a short ball just remember you're fine at the line.

227 Sometimes Forehand, Sometimes Backhand

As I mentioned previously, rarely are both your forehand and backhand on for the entire match. When you find that a particular shot isn't feeling strong, first figure out what kind of shots your opponent is hitting to you. You might be giving your opponent a shot they like and then you have to deal with a defensive shot. Also recognize that sometimes you have to play defense for a while until your good feeling shot comes back. Rather than forcing offense that isn't there, you need to forget about winning and focus on making shots. It's okay to play defense! Keeping the ball in play puts pressure on your opponents so you can win even when you aren't hitting well.

228 It's the Distance Not Your Skill

Mary, Alex and Paulette all have great forehands, yet in the last week, all three ladies hit down-the-line forehands that hit the tape on the net. They were all frustrated to miss their offensive shots in the net. I explained that it wasn't their skills but it was a distance issue. The ladies tried to hit down-the-line from behind the baseline. The net is six inches higher over the alleys, which makes that a bit more difficult. If you are inside the baseline, it is a better time to hit down-the-line.

229 Battle Like a Boxer

If you watch the highlights of any boxing match you usually see two or three decent punches followed by the big knockout punch. What you don't see on the highlights are the many jabs that make up the back and forth battle. Tennis is just the same. Think back to your last match. How many winners did you hit? Let's say that you and your partner hit a dozen winners. That's a decent amount but you also had to win another thirty-six points to win the match in its entirety. How did you win those points? The majority of points are lost or finished by an error. In fact, 70% of all points at the professional level are ended in error. It's the solid, high-percentage play, rather than an occasional winner, that wins in tennis.

The Backhand You Want

If you don't like your backhand, that's okay. You just need to show your opponent that you can make your backhand shots rather than making it a weapon. If you are right handed and don't like your backhand it's better to play the ad side when you return serve. When you stand close to the alley you are covering a large area on your backhand side. Don't worry about the opening down the T because your opponent usually isn't skilled enough to hit a hard serve down the T to ace you. If they do serve down the T, you will be moving to hit your forehand. If they serve out wide and you have to hit your backhand, you will have a crosscourt angle lined up. This is the backhand you want! As an added bonus, you are hitting towards your opponent's backhand.

The Third Partner

Your third partner isn't a player, it is the sun. When you are playing on a clear, sunny day, the sun will be bad on one side of the court. It's a smart idea to take that sunny side during warm-ups so you can get used to the sun in your eyes. When you switch sides after the first game, your opponents will be in the sun for two games. You should lob them several times, forcing them to look into the sun. When you return back onto the sunny side and they lob you, let their lob bounce so that you aren't looking into the sun. Everyone needs some extra Vitamin D, so give it to them early and often.

232 What Do You Say When...

What do you say when your partner is bad? They aren't just bad, but they're missing many shots and costing you points. Certainly you want to help them by saying something, but to be a good and effective doubles partner you must first remember your job. Your job is to make your returns and be as solid as you can. Your partner's mistakes are only worth one point so let it go and focus on what you can do. Feel free to say a word of encouragement if that might help, but never mention their mistakes. Say something like, "Hey, shake it off, you got this," or, "I know you're a solid player so just one point at a time." You can also subtly give your partner some advice by telling them what strategies or adjustments you're going to make. Remember to hang tough and give yourself and your partner time to pull it together.

233 Six in a Row?

Two high level players, Chris and Paul, were doubles partners recently. They won their match despite having a rough first set. They shared a conversation they had during that rough first set. Chris complained to Paul saying, "I've missed five forehands in a row!" Paul looked straight at Chris and said, "Well you sure as h*** won't miss six!" What great wisdom from Paul. Think about it. When was the last time you've missed six in a row? Actually, don't think about it. We keep track of these mistakes in our heads during the match and that puts unnecessary pressure on ourselves. Your opponents don't know how many you missed in a row; they are just happy to be winning. The next time you miss a few in a row, have a talk with yourself and remember the odds are in your favor that you will make the next shot.

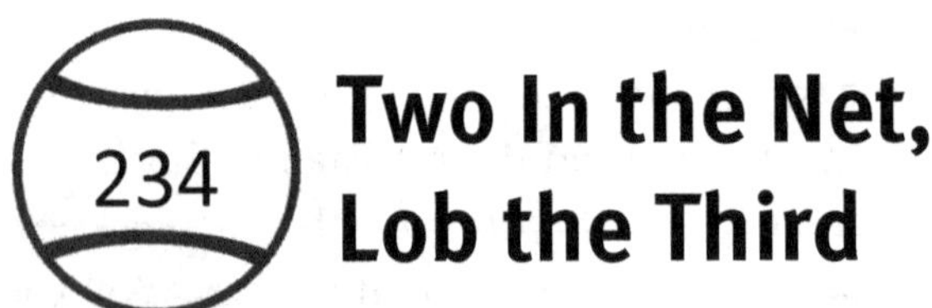

234 Two In the Net, Lob the Third

This is one of those unwritten rules you should follow. When you hit two consecutive groundstrokes into the net, your next shot should be a lob. You might recover from losing two points, but losing three is almost a given that you will lose the game. When you lob, you are at least beating the net and keeping the ball in play. On your next groundstroke, maintain the feeling of lifting your shot from the previous lob. By lobbing you are slowing the match down which gives you the time to change your losing game. Remember two in the net, lob the third.

I'm Thinking Too Much!

An easy ball while you are in an offensive position gives you many options. In this case, that's a good thing because you have set the point up in your favor. However, players often miss easy shots because they think too much. They think about how many options or targets they have, or get excited because they assume that they will definitely win the point. Several points after my player, Jane, said, "I'm thinking too much," she hit a strong shot through the middle between her opponents. I then asked her what she was thinking. She said she was just aiming down the middle. That's the way you should play. Play with a picture in your mind of where you intend to hit your shot. Keep your thoughts simple and the rest will follow.

236 That Was In, Right?

When you aren't sure if your shot was in or out, what do you ask your opponent? If you ask if your shot was in or out, what do you think they will likely say? They want it to be out and if you give them that option, they'll likely decide out. Asking lets them know that you are questioning if your shot was in. The next time your opponent hesitates calling your shot, simply ask them, "That was *in,* right?" Now you sound like you have confidence that your shot was definitely in. Never, ever give them the option to decide that your shot was out. You intended to hit it in so believe it was in. Also next time, don't hit so close to the line!

237 Try Two Hands

No, I'm not talking about two hands on your backhand groundstroke. I'm talking about your forehand volley. Take ready position up at the net with your racket out in front of you. Now make a backhand volley. Notice on your backhand volley that your hand is out in front of your body. That's exactly where you want to make your point of contact.

Now shadow a forehand volley. With this shot, players

tend to pull the elbow close to their side which makes the contact point too close to your body. Now try putting your non-dominant hand above your dominant hand on your grip then reach forward with both hands and make a fore-hand volley. You will notice that your racket is out in front of your body. The next time you're on the court, have your partner feed you a few volleys and start with the two-handed forehand volley. After you make a few, volley with just one hand and see if you have your contact out in front.

238 Hit It In the Blue

This will help you when you feel like you are hitting too many balls late. Before you overanalyze your stroke, try to make your contact point earlier. If you were looking at yourself from the side, you would see where you made your contact. When you are late, your contact point is be-hind the baseline. Aim to hit the ball earlier while the ball is in the blue. You want to strike the ball before it crosses the baseline. Making your contact in front of yourself is proactive and takes the focus away from preventing your-self from being late.

239 What's Their Pattern?

The next time you lose a point, immediately ask yourself, "What did they just do?" You might have missed the last shot but what shot did they hit just before you missed? Where did they serve when the serve was at deuce? Which direction do they typically return? If you discuss these patterns with your partner, you can anticipate their tendencies as the match progresses. You won't be correct 100% of the time, but you might catch onto their patterns early enough to change the outcome of a set or even the match. Keep asking questions about your opponents and the answers will come.

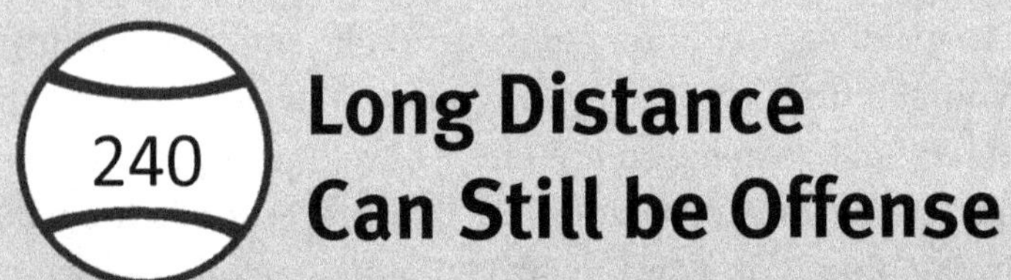

240 Long Distance Can Still be Offense

You are several feet behind the baseline and your opponent hits a deep ball. Distance-wise, you are on defense because of how far away you are from the net. However, you can still be aggressive from deep behind the baseline. Go ahead and rip a very aggressive groundstroke and add some height to it because you never miss in the net. You aren't going for a winner, but you are trying to hit a forceful shot. Your opponent believes you are going to hit a safe, loopy shot or high return just to be safe. You'll likely surprise them with such an aggressive shot. If the opponent in front of you is up at the net and doesn't volley well, there's a chance they will miss your aggressive shot or make a weak volley.

241 Try Some Hammers

If you want to feel comfortable with the continental grip, try some hammers. Hammers are where you bounce the ball on the ground with the edge of your racket. It mirrors the feeling of hammering something. Try doing some hammers with your forehand grip, then some with the continental grip. After practicing hammers, immediately hit some backhands. You should feel more comfortable using the continental grip on your backhand. The more you use the continental grip on your backhand, the better it will become because you have practiced closing the racket face.

242 Just Push It

Too often on the return of serve, players will take too big of a swing. It's natural to try to catch up to the speed of your opponent's fast serve. However, taking a big backswing followed by a fast swing on your return makes timing the fast serve very difficult. Believe it or not, that is more of a mental mistake than a physical one. Rather than trying to make a great return to a fast serve, push your return crosscourt and get it back into play. Make a unit turn with your shoulders and keep your racket close to you. Then focus on making contact in front of your body. You can absorb the pace the server supplied to block or push it back. When you get a high percentage of returns in play, it is very frustrating for a dominant server. They will tend to over-hit and drop their percentage helping you out!

243 Brutal Truth

There will be days in your tennis career that you are just bad! It happens to all of us. Hopefully when you have one of those days, your partner will be very solid and consistent. After you play on a day when you stink, you don't have to dwell on your performance, just flush away all thoughts about your bad day. A couple of ladies I coach told me about their bad day involving some not-so-nice opponents. I instructed them to go home and write their opponents' names on a tissue. Then I told them to go into their bathrooms and stand in front of the toilet. They were told to verbalize everything they hated about their match, then crumple up the tissue and flush it down the toilet! If needed, literally flush all the negative thoughts about your opponents and your performance on the court away after your match. Forget about the bad days and keep on playing. Big picture thinking here… you have two working legs so go out and play as much as you can!

244 Have You Ever?

Have you ever been in your house and gone over to your racket bag and pulled out one of your rackets? Then did you grab your grip, smile, and think, "Ah! I love how my racket feels in my hand!" Then perhaps you started swinging forehands and backhands at an imaginary ball. Then you picture where you will be playing tomorrow, and for a second you put on your game face. You have total focus and total intensity in preparation. Hall of Fame basketball player, Bill Walton, once said, "I was so grateful that I used to wake up in the morning and know that I was going to kick someone's ass on the basketball court that day. Now I'm too old and can't play." I have good news for Bill. There's an age division and an ability level division for everyone in tennis, especially here in the ATL!

245 I Keep Getting Lobbed!

Before you complain about losing a point or anything your opponent is doing that you don't like, you should ask yourself several questions.

1. Did you hit it directly to them?
2. Did they hit a forehand or backhand?

3. Were they running or stationary?
4. Were they on offense or defense?
5. Where were you standing?
6. What type of shot did I send to them?
7. Was your opponent fortunate or just lucky?
8. Can your opponent do that same shot consistently?
9. Should I vary the amount of times I approach?
10. Is your opponent moving forward or backward to lob you?

There are other questions and clues as to why they are lobbing you. Answering these questions will provide you with some answers to understand why you are receiving so many lobs. Play the percentages and if you can make any shot challenging for your opponents, they won't win by hitting many winners.

Connect with Your Partner

The easiest part of a point is the high five or fist bump you share with your partner after making that point. What about when you or your partner miss an easy shot on a crucial point? You might not want to even look at your partner after that, but the important thing to remember is that you are a doubles team. Team stands for Together Everyone Achieves More! When you both come together and talk, for even a few seconds, you will feel like you are competing as a team. Use some encouraging phrases to help you and your partner compete better. Remember that the past is gone and you two are now moving on to the next point. You can also discuss strategy by telling them where you plan to serve or return so that they can anticipate the next shot. A bonus of connecting between points is that your opponents may think you're changing your strategy and overthink their actions. I don't care if you tell a joke, vent, or don't even say anything. Just connect for 3-5 seconds between every point. Even walk to the bench and switch sides together so you compete as a T.E.A.M.

247 Five Screws

One of the greatest minds and leaders of research in the tennis field was the late Vic Braden. One of the findings in Vic's research revealed that, on average, your opponent will miss at least five calls per match. Having this discussion about line calls with one of my men's teams, we came up with a saying that helps them whenever their opponents miss a call that was obviously in. We named it the Five Screws. The men realized that they would get "screwed" out of at least five points per match. Of course, we could be wrong, but knowing five calls on average won't be in your favor can help you deal with it when it does happen. The solution for this team was when it does happen, they say to each other, "Screw one." When it happens again, they look at each other and say, "Screw two," and so on. This way they don't engage in an argument and just let the point go. Oftentimes when your opponent is missing calls, you are hitting too close to the lines. Give yourself a bigger target and you won't be in danger of losing so many points.

248 Play Your Style but Mix It Up

You might be an aggressive player that returns any weak shot and then rushes the net. Or you could be a solid baseliner that sets up your partner and can outlast exhausting opponents. Your style might be very successful but there is a risk in sticking with your style the entire match. It's true that you don't want to change a winning game, but the risk lies in the possibility that your opponents will get used to your style and get comfortable. More points in tennis are decided by an error. When you mix up your style, your opponents can't find a rhythm. You want to continue your style for about 75-80% of the time. For example, you are serving down the T and your opponent misses their backhand or returns it weak. An occasional serve out wide to their forehand will keep them off balance. They assume that the serve will go down the T but you change it up and go wide. From the baseline you should throw in an occasional lob if you've been driving most of your shots. Have fun mixing it up and seeing how many different ways you can make your opponents miss!

Bling or the Bird

At some point, usually as a beginner, you will have problems controlling your toss. You might flick your wrist or throw the toss rather than placing the ball in your hitting zone. I tell the ladies to pretend you are lifting your big diamond (the bling) up as you toss. I tell the men that as they toss they should pretend they are shooting "the bird" at their opponent. You want to have a slow, lifting motion when you toss. The slower the better so you can get a consistent placement of your toss.

Zero Spin on the Toss

Does even the thought of tossing the ball create some anxiety in you? The majority of problems with the serve are because of an errant toss. Wrist flick, bending the elbow, fast arm motions, and throwing the ball instead of lifting are all causes of an unreliable toss. The ball is very light which makes it important to have a slow motion to maintain your control. To calm down your movements and make a consistent placement of your toss, practice lifting the ball so that it has zero spin while it goes up in the air. Toss it as slow as possible so that it looks like it's still while it's in the air. You can do it! Go slow, then slower, then even slower. Once the toss is in its place you can let it rip with your contact.

251 See the Bounce

If you have ever experienced playing on a grass court, you know the ball bounces lower compared to a hard or clay court. At my first grass court tournament, I noticed many players were hitting the ball off of their frames on their groundstrokes. This was because they kept the same posture that they would have used on a hard or clay court. When someone hits a slice to you the ball skids and stays lower than the typical topspin shot. The key to staying down on a slice or low bouncing shot, is to first see the bounce. Rather than tracking after the bounce, literally try to see where the ball hits the court. Your body naturally follows your eyes and seeing the ball bounce will help you stay down and handle the low bounce.

252 Either Great or Garbage

You haven't played in a while. It could have been a few weeks, a month, or even longer. So how do you hit when you get back out on the courts? When back from a hiatus, you are either great or garbage. You could be great because you don't have high expectations for your performance. Low expectations help you relax and hit well. The other scenario after a layoff is that your game is just garbage. Your timing is bad, your feet are slow, you aren't tracking the ball well and it's just a brutal time on the court. Here's where you can just relax and know that the more frequently you play, the better you'll be.

Exhale on Your Effort

Have you ever felt strained to pick up something heavy? When you strain to do something, there's a natural release of your breath as you complete it. Believe it or not, it is encouraged to breathe out as you hit. The noises you hear on TV are a bit exaggerated, I agree, but here's what I want you to try. Next time you practice or take a lesson, breathe out as you hit. You can even make it audible if you need to. Notice how it makes you relax. When you hold your breath your body gets tense and that can make your contact feel tight and rigid. When you exhale on your hit, you will relax and also play better!

254 Intensity!

The most intense athlete I have ever seen is Kevin Garnett, but is intensity good for a tennis player? One might say that it worked for Jimmy Connors, John McEnroe, and Rafael Nadal. The intensity that most people think about comes from the mental side or a player's emotional state. There's nothing wrong with being more intense than your teammates and your opponents. Whatever it takes to help you play your best is the way you should compete. Limiting the physical intensity is something most players don't think about. The only intensity I want you to have, physically, is with your lower body. Bend, lunge, quickly move your feet, push off, turn and run, explode to the ball, and never stop moving while the ball is in play. Be the best mover on the court. If you aren't hitting well, up the intensity with your footwork and move more. The intensity that is counterproductive comes with your upper body. You want to relax your shoulders, arms, and grip pressure. Think about a time when you hit a really good serve or groundstroke. Your upper body probably felt very relaxed and your shot was almost effortless. The ultimate player has great footwork with smooth swings. Keep your upper body loose and bring the intensity with your lower body.

255 Hero or High Percentage?

The score is 4-All, deuce, and you are returning from the deuce side. Your opponent serves out wide to your forehand. Where are you going to return the first serve? Will you hit crosscourt with a high percentage shot, or will you go for a winner down-the-line and be a hero? You might want to consider this before you choose. The hero wins sometimes, but the high percentage player wins most of the time. You could try to show off your strong forehands and be a hero, but if you miss, your partner will be facing game point against you. If you're winning by two points and have an easy shot to work with, you can go for the hero shot. Otherwise, be smart and play the high percentage crosscourt.

256 What Are the Odds of Three in a Row?

You come to the net on your approach shot or you are the net player when your partner is serving. The opposing baseliner returns the ball and you volley it back because the shot was so hard you couldn't angle it away from them. They then return it towards you again. You can't angle this one either, but you do volley it towards the middle. Now think for a second. What are the odds that your opponent will make a third groundstroke? Even though you haven’t put the volley away for a winner, you are still in an offensive position. Your opponent just ripped two groundstrokes in a row and you returned both of them. At this point in the rally they will usually be frustrated. It’s likely that they will hit the second shot harder than the first shot, and the third will be harder than the second. It’s doubtful they will retain control while hitting harder and harder. Stay steady and solid at the net and if they happen to make three in a row, then just remember you returned their last two shots and you still have an offensive position.

You’re Okay at 18 Feet

The distance from the baseline to the net is 39 feet. Most people think that the service line is halfway to the net. If you look at the court from an aerial view, you will see that the service line is closer to the baseline. When you get to the service line, you have moved 18 feet. Now you have 21 more feet to go to reach the net. You’re not running a foot race to the net, however. You are just moving in, which immediately puts pressure on your opponents. If you stop your approach at the service line, you will have plenty of time to cover their lob. Remember that the service line is 3 feet closer to the baseline. If your opponent drives the ball at you, move forward to volley. You are moving forward so you will at least be halfway into the service box when you do volley. There are times when your opponents are dipping their shots into the service box, so when this happens, you need to move past the service line. It is important to always remember that tennis is situational and you have to make adjustments.

500 Serves This Month

Junior players and adults will often put in extra practice to improve their serves. They usually take their basket out and hit 100-200 serves on a Saturday afternoon. The only problem they have is that they've lost the feeling they felt by Tuesday. The best way to get your serve automatic and developed into a weapon is to hit 500 serves in the next month. The good news is that it only takes about ten minutes a day. So here's your homework or better, your opportunity. Twenty-five serves, Monday through Friday, means you will serve 125 serves per week. In four weeks, those 125 serves become 500 serves! You can totally do this! Just one month of dedication to improve the most important shot in tennis!

Think It's In!

Imagine a baseball pitcher getting the sign from his catcher. Before he throws his pitch, do you think he wonders if he will throw a strike? Of course not! He believes he's going to throw the pitch exactly where he wants to throw it. You should think the same way, especially when you serve. If you decide you're going to serve down the T, then when you toss, the only picture in your mind is your serve going *in* towards the T. When you picture any shot going in, you'll relax and execute it better. Overthinking about the score, winning the point, or how you are hitting the shot, puts unnecessary pressure on yourself. Keep your thoughts simple!

260 The Towel Game

The next time you and your partner are practicing together there's a game you should play to work on your placement. Take your towel and place it halfway between the service line and baseline. Have your partner put their towel in the same space on their side of the court. Now rally and try to hit the towel on your partner's side of the court. The game goes to three. After one of you hits the towel three times, put the towels on the ad side of the court. You will notice two things in particular when you play the towel game. You get the feel and control of hitting to a specific area on the court and you and your partner will become more consistent. Your consistency increases because you are working on direction, rather than speed. My buddy, Howard, and I invented the towel game and it's an awesome way to get a focused warm up.

261 Going Deep

Here, we are talking about breaking your opponent's serve. You are up 30-40, breakpoint. The server wins the next point and it's deuce. You proceed to have a forever deuce game in which you have four or five breakpoints. However, your opponent holds the serve. You didn't break serve despite all of those chances. Do not let that get you down! You just went deep into your opponent's service game. I guarantee during some of your breakpoints that your opponent felt pressure. What do you think they will feel the next time they are serving 30-All or deuce? Yes, they'll feel pressure. Eventually when you continue to go deep into their service games, they will crumble under the pressure, and you will break their serve.

262 Hitters and Players

As you drive up to your match, your opponents are already on the court hitting. They look great. Uh oh! You immediately think you're in trouble and might lose today. Relax! Your opponents are hitting comfortable shots. You must remember that hitting in practice is different from playing. When the match starts you will see how they play with different shots. There's a huge difference between the casual warm-up and the consequences of losing when you miss a shot. Pay attention to how your opponents play when you hit your strong shots. How do they play when they are on defense? How do they play when you are in the lead? All of these elements of competition affect the way players play. Anyone can look good hitting an easy shot, but real players play well when they have to compete.

263 Winners Don't Win

I want you to hit as many winners as you can. Realize that to win a match you need to win 24 points a set for two sets. That's only 48 points. After we discuss winners with my players, we discuss how they forced errors from their opponents. I also applaud them when they tell me about the adjustments they made when they realized how their opponent was hurting them. Go ahead and hit the winners if you are able to, otherwise stay steady and make it difficult on your opponents.

264 Can They Maintain It?

You and your partner just lost the first set 6-0 in about fifteen minutes. Your opponents only lost five points the entire set. They were serving huge and ripping winners. You and your partner sit down on the changeover and shrug your shoulders because you don't have a clue what to do. You can't control how well they serve, but you and your partner can play two-back on their serves. You can vary your positioning when you are the serving team. You can lob more. You can hit slower. You want to try as many different things as you can to prolong the match. Your opponents might be having a career day and you might lose, but your goal should be to find some way to make it difficult for them to maintain their high level. It is difficult for someone to hit great for two hours. One of the greatest things about tennis is that you have all day to make your comeback. There's no clock that can expire on you. Find a way!

This Isn't Gymnastics

Too often tennis players want to look good or hit in a way that's technically correct. Tennis isn't like gymnastics, diving, dance, or ice skating. There are no points or deductions for technical merit or how elegant you are. This is a battle to put one more ball back in play and make your opponent miss their shot. Technique matters to help produce quality shots, but there are situations where you just have to find a way to put the ball in play regardless of your form. Linda was poaching and she hit the ball with her frame and it dropped in for a winner. Carolyn hit a running backhand lob that landed on her opponent's baseline. Both Linda and Carolyn said they didn't know how they hit their winners. It didn't matter how they hit them or their technique. They got the ball IN!

266 Drop Shot Mistake

You have your opponent running off the court and they return your shot short in the service box. You are in the perfect situation to hit a drop shot. You can almost hear the applause from the fans watching when you hit your beautiful drop shot winner but then it happens... your drop shot hits the tape and falls back on your side of the court. The mistake is trying to hit a winner. Your goal is to win the point, not to make the highlight reel. If you execute your drop shot into your opponent's service box, they will have to run a long way just to reach it. They will be lifting the ball up giving you or your partner a nice high easy ball should he even make it over the net. Instead of hitting a winner, remember to make a difficult shot for your opponent. The bonus is when they missed their shot, not only did you make them run, but they will be angry they missed. This way you win twice!

267 Whenever You Can

You're up at the net and your partner is great at the baseline so you're not sure if you should poach or let them hit their groundstroke. Poach whenever you can. But what about other times like with a short ball that bounces in your partner's service box? Should you get it or should you let your partner move up from the baseline and take it? What you need to consider is if you think your partner won't make it up to the ball, then you should go get it. The most important thing to remember is that when you go get the ball, you are taking time away from your opponent. If you let your partner run up from the baseline to get the ball, your opponents are expecting that and have plenty of time to react. If you can get it and cause problems for your opponent, then go get it whenever you can.

268 Move On

All players have been in a long rally and played incredibly, only to lose the point. You feel like you invested so much but received nothing for your efforts. It becomes even more frustrating when playing in the heat. A common mistake after losing a long point is to press on the following point to make up for one you just lost. All points in tennis are only worth one point, win or lose. The President of Basketball Operations for the Boston Celtics, Brad Stevens, has a great definition for mental toughness: "Mental toughness is the ability to go from play to play without getting too high or too low depending on the results." That's what I want you to do. Keep up your intensity, focus, and move on to the next point. I received a great text recently from one of my players named Dawn. "I did what you told me - play the point, left it behind when it was over, and then focused on getting the opponents out of their comfort zones, *and* I had fun playing one point at a time!" Good work Dawn! Way to be mentally tough!

269 Sampras Would Have Ripped That Forehand!

Pam was on the run returning Lisa's sliced angled forehand. Pam did a great job of getting to the ball. She lobbed it up but Debbie made a successful overhead. Pam thought she should have done more with her running forehand. I told her that she gave a great effort, but was on defense so Lisa earned the point. Pete Sampras on the other hand, would have ripped a crosscourt winner. Federer might have done the same thing. Unfortunately we "mortal" tennis players compare or try to live up to what we see on TV. Modeling the professionals' great fundamentals and tactics are great starting points, but asking yourself to do something that the pros do is unrealistic and unfair to yourself. Stay solid and hang tough while letting the pros create the highlight reel.

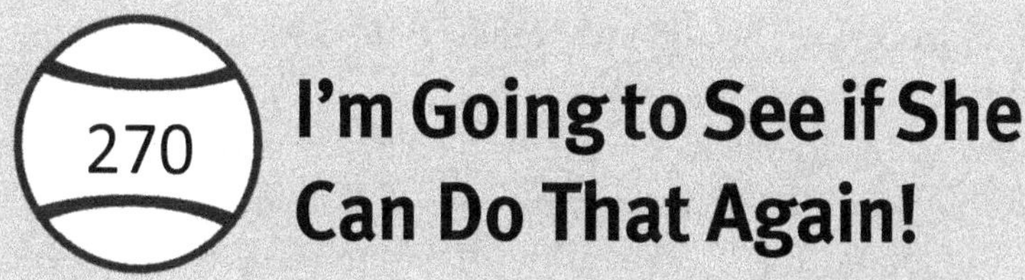

270 I'm Going to See if She Can Do That Again!

At practice, Angel hit an amazing backhand crosscourt winner. She has a very good backhand. After Angel hit her winner, on the very next point Pam took the short ball and attacked Angel's backhand. Pam hit a good approach shot that made Angel hit a neutral ball instead of an aggressive shot. When Pam won the point, she looked at Sarah and said, "I'm going to see if she can do that again!" What a great mindset! Your opponents will definitely hit some winners against you. Some opponents just have weapons that are hard to deal with. Just because they have a weapon doesn't mean they will always hit winners. When you change speeds, adjust your court position, or attack them when the score is close, they might buckle under the pressure and miss. Have the attitude that no one can hit winners for two hours against you. Find ways to mix it up and I doubt they will!

271 What's Your Least Favorite Shot?

Do you dislike running for a drop shot? Do you hate hitting a running backhand? How do you like returning the lob that went over your partner's head that lands deep and bounces high? Do you like to receive a drive or a loopy ball from your opponent? Nancy and Laura told me about a recent match they played. Their opponents were strong and didn't seem to have any weaknesses so they didn't know what to do. When you're in a similar situation just think about the shots you don't like to receive. The shots you don't like to hit might be the kind of shots your opponents don't like to hit either. Even if an opponent returns a shot that you think is difficult, at least you didn't make the point easy for them. Watch their body language as well and keep looking for clues to find the shots they don't like to hit.

272 Feed Yourself

A great way to develop feel and control on your groundstrokes is to feed yourself. Stand at the baseline, drop the ball, and hit. One good drill that will really help your doubles is to work on your topspin dipper. Bounce the ball and try to hit a crosscourt dipper into the service box. A dipper is a shot with heavy topspin that dips rapidly into the court. You gain feel because you are putting all the spin and speed onto your shot. You can also work on your slice by feeding yourself. Try tossing the ball a few feet in front of you to simulate an approach shot. After feeding yourself and gaining confidence you will be ready to face the oncoming shots from your opponents knowing you have the feel to execute your shots!

273 Lob the Lights

You are running off the court and your best option is to lob the ball, but you are so defensive that your lob has no chance of going over the net player's head. You are also afraid that your opponent will slam the overhead at your partner. Your best strategy in this situation is to lob the ball as high as you can. Aim above the lights. You should follow through towards the lights to make sure your lob is high. The height of the ball will buy your partner precious milliseconds of reaction time. The high lob will also be difficult for your opponent to track and take out of the air.

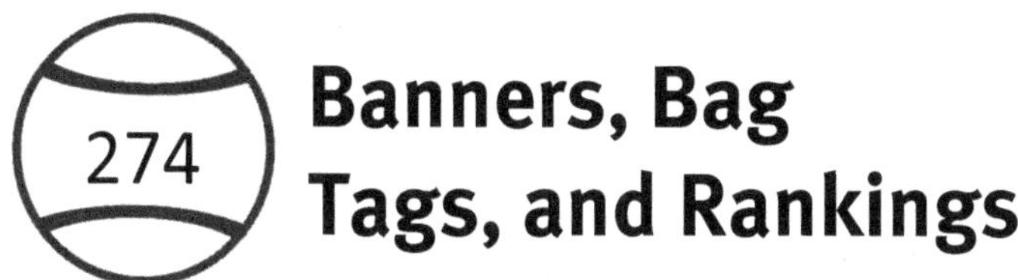

274 Banners, Bag Tags, and Rankings

You are walking up to your court and you see Division Winner and Championship banners all over the fences. Your opponent's bag is clanking because of all of their bag tags. You also just found out that several of their players hold state rankings because they play in tournaments. *So what*? Banners, bag tags, and state rankings just mean they have been successful in the past. It could even mean that they were just on really good teams. Turn this observation into a positive optimistic outlook for you and your partner. Those players that have won so much in the past feel more pressure because they hate telling people they lost. They may feel the need to live up to all those bag tags and banners. Think this way. If you lose, then you lost to a good team. However, you should think that the closer the match score gets, and the longer the match goes, they will be the ones facing the pressure. Past performances don't give them any future points.

275 Change Your Toss?

You might have heard an instructor tell a student, "You should toss to the side more if you want to get more slice on your serve. Then, if you want more kick on your serve, toss more over your head." Now picture yourself as the returner. After seeing different tosses, you can then predict what type of serve is about to hit. Now picture yourself as the server. How long did it take you to develop a consistent and reliable toss? And now to add some spin you need to have a different toss as well? That's not a wise move. You can learn a strong slice serve by starting with a continental grip. You can also develop a kick serve by hitting from 7 to 2 on the ball. You can try to manipulate the racket head and your hand and see what spin you can generate. Most importantly, have a toss that is placed in a position that allows you to serve consistently. Stick with one toss!

276 History

This won't be a grand discussion on who is the greatest player in history. If you want to have that conversation, let me know and I'll buy the first round. To be a great player and be mentally tough, you must forget about your screw ups! Each point is only worth *one point*. It doesn't matter that you double faulted the game away, that you poached on game point and missed by three feet, or that you had an overhead on set point and then you choked! Well guess what… you're not alone! Play long enough and that will happen to you at some point. When you screw up, you need to remember that the last point you just played is history. Good or bad you must move on to the next point. If you get burned by your opponent, remember what shot they hit or what shot you gave to them to set up their strong shot. You have to put the emotions of the last shot in the past. Keep fighting and you might be the ones who make history with your comeback!

277 V for Victory

Make a peace sign with your first two fingers. Now visualize you are standing in the middle of the service box. Put the peace sign out in front of you. You can now see your path and the best way to poach and cut off your opponent's passing shots. When you move on a V, you are moving diagonally and this is the quickest way to meet the ball. The typical mistake is to move laterally. Lateral starts with "L" which also stands for "Loser!" Think V for victory and you will poach like a net monster!

278 A Repeatable Speed

Have you ever hit a winner then struggled to hit the same shot again? There's a possibility that the winner you hit was so powerful that it was too hard to hit again. The good news is that you hit a winner. It doesn't have to be hit with power, it just needs to be out of your opponent's reach. Three men that I coach hit more than an average amount of winners per match. Lefties Marc and Aaron have lethal one handed backhands and Charlie is right-handed and can rip winners with both his forehand and his backhand. The important fundamental these men consistently apply is hitting with a repeatable speed, rather than hitting so hard their shots are all or nothing. Forget about winners and think about hitting a shot that goes in consistently where you want it to go. You can add power, just make sure you're hitting a repeatable speed!

One Goal

You should have one goal in mind before you play your match. There are outcome goals and there are performance goals. A possible outcome goal would be to win at least 80% of your matches during the season. Whereas one example of a performance goal would be that you're going to hit topspin on every backhand during the match. Performance goals are those that improve your chances of achieving your outcome goals. Before your next match, have a performance goal in mind. Here are a few examples of performance goals:

> "I'm going to make every volley solid with great focus, especially on easy volleys."
> "I'm going to keep my head still on my returns and groundstrokes."
> "I'm going to reach up on all my serves."

You can change your performance goals from match to match depending on the area that you want to improve. If you missed too many first serves last match you might want to add more spin on your first serve to get your percentages up. You tend to get what you focus on so set a performance goal before every match.

75%

If you were back in school, you probably would think 75% is a bad thing. However, 75% in tennis is great! Wouldn't you like to make 75% of your first serves? How about returning 75% of your opponents serves? A few years ago, my friend Howard gave me an article written by Dr. Bryce Young PhD. One tip in his article said, "Hit with 75% of your power and the ball will go in 75% of the time." Many players tend to believe that hitting hard is better and they may just like to hit the ball hard. Nearly all players have wanted to hit a hard shot because it's impressive. A few powerful crowd pleasers are okay, but winning teams know that high-percentage is more important than power. The next time you serve, try to hit with 75% of your power and see how your percentages are. If you're up 40-Love and want to crank it up, then that's okay. Otherwise follow the 75% rule.

Your Feet

"You are where your feet are," is a great quote by Nick Saban. Coach Saban's quote is in reference to being in the moment. He teaches playing one play at a time without dwelling on the last play or thinking about what's coming in the next. Should you lose a point in tennis and not like the way you played the point, I want you to think about moving your feet more for the next point. Usually, when you make an error in tennis, it is because of your feet. Eighty percent of all errors are footwork related. Remember to focus on moving your feet more and stay in the moment. Judging by his results, Coach Saban knows what he's talking about!

282 When You Press, They Press

One way of looking at rushing the net is just like a press in basketball. Coach Andy Akin and Coach Dwight Ellenburg instilled in us at West Rome High School that good defense would make winning easier. Rushing the net in tennis is like defense in other sports. Your defense makes it difficult on your opponents, which makes winning easier for you. A press in basketball is an aggressive defensive strategy that creates turnovers from the other team. When you rush the net, you are pressing forward. When your opponents see you rush the net, they often rush their groundstrokes because you made them feel like they didn't have much time. This also forces mistakes from your opponents. You are applying pressure when you come in and nobody wants to face pressure. When you press, they press. Press them early and often!

Kill That Cockroach!

Have you ever had a cockroach in your house? What was your first instinct? Step on that bug! This will help you be a better net player. There are 3 strategies while playing the net that will help you win more points:

1. GO! When you see their return go get it.
2. Fake! When the ball bounces, fake like you are going.
3. Fake early, then GO!

Some people think to fake you must move three feet, then move back. That's too far to go and you don't have time to move that much. Try this instead. When the ball bounces on your opponent's side of the court, take one, hard step towards the middle like you are stepping on a cockroach. Your big step will definitely make your opponent think you are poaching. Your goal is to distract the returner with that big and loud step. Don't worry if they make their return. Keep stepping to the middle and faking, and you will force errors from the returner.

The Long Term Effect

When players line up in the I-formation and lose the point, they mistakenly stop doing it. One of the main purposes of the I-formation is to break the return pattern of the return team. The return team is on auto-pilot to return crosscourt when you are in the conventional formation. When you line up in the I-formation, the returner might go crosscourt, down-the-line or lob. What's most important is that the returner must now think about the movement of the net player and counter that with their return. When practicing the I-formation to the ad side, Suzy, Susie, Pam, and Lisa understood the long term effect on the return team. I made them play I-formation on every point to the ad side. Try it the next time you are serving at 15-30. This is such an important point for the serving team because you don't want to lose and be down 15-40. It takes courage to try a new or uncomfortable position so remember your opponents aren't comfortable with your changing of formations either. The long term effect will benefit you and your partner.

The Dreaded Floater

Your opponent either mishits or intentionally lobs to you while you are at the baseline. You know that the ball is going to bounce high, and because you are behind the baseline, you know it will be a defensive shot. There are two ways to handle the floater. You can step back and let the ball drop down into a comfortable strike zone, or move into no-man's-land and volley the ball out of the air. All you are trying to do on the floater is to send it back until you have an easier ball to play. The major mistake is to be impatient and play too aggressively. Remember that you didn't like receiving the floater, so give them a high bouncing floater right back at them.

286 No Switching

Often during a team practice, I will tell the serving team that if their opponents lob them, they are not allowed to switch to cover the lob. They usually think I'm crazy or unrealistic. You can surprise yourself by seeing just how much distance you can cover when you are determined to reach their lob. The most important step is to turn *immediately* when you see the ball is a lob. Turn towards the ball, either over your right or left shoulder. Now the mistake is thinking that you're going to hit an overhead off of their lob. You might not be able to hit an overhead, but you may be able to block the lob back into play. Blocking the ball out of the air benefits you in three ways. For starters, you are returning the ball to your opponents faster. Secondly, you stop the chaos of switching when your partner has to hit a running, deep and high bouncing shot. Thirdly, the opponent that lobbed you will get discouraged that their lob didn't get over your head even if you just frame it and miss. Commit to getting every lob with no switching and see how many you can get.

287 It Was Effective Even If You Lost

You lobbed the net player. They turned and took three steps beyond the service line and made an amazing, scissor kick overhead. Unbelievably, they hit a deep overhead through the middle of the court for a winner. Before you decide to never lob again, realize how far back your lob pushed the net player. If your lob pushes the net player beyond the service line it is a good lob! So what if they made an amazing shot, you still made the shot difficult for them. Keep making your opponent hit difficult shots and they will make plenty of errors. If your lob pushes them back, they will usually start deeper in the service box which puts them farther away from a poach. Your lob doesn't have to go over their heads to be effective. Just push them back!

You're Going to Lose a Bunch!

How's that for some encouraging advice? I'm just going to give it to you straight. Research done by Craig O'Shaughnessy has shown that the #1 player in the world loses close to 45% of the points he plays. All you need to do is win 51% of the points. If you lost 6-1,6-1, but most games went to deuce, you might at least feel that the match was close even if the score didn't indicate that. Now when you win a match 7-5, 6-4, do you really think about how many points you lost afterwards? You could have gone to deuce many times during your close victory, but you won the crucial two points in a row at deuce and you didn't worry about the points you lost. The bottom line is that you have to keep playing mini-games, 2 points at a time in your head. Reset after each game and focus on what you can control. The points you lost are in the past.

Try This!

You are playing someone who has a big serve. You and your partner are stuck with how to get it back into play. Here's what I want you to try. On the next changeover, immediately after your opponent serves, ask this, "You have such a great serve! How do you hit it so big?" Then shut-up, walk to your bench, and act like you never asked anything. They will puff out their chest and likely not give you any secrets. However, what they will think about your compliment, strutting around with the thought that they can't wait to serve again. Now here's what will probably happen. They will be thinking about your compliment and try to live up to it and exceed it. They might hit a couple more bombs but drop their percentage considerably. Your opponent is going to overthink and try too hard to live up to their past big serves. This can also work by complimenting any shot. Try it! You have nothing to lose!!

290 "I Can't Believe... "

If you're like most players, you don't prefer your backhand over your forehand. Your backhand might not be weak, but you definitely don't consider it a weapon. Here's something that will help you receive more forehands during your match. The next time you miss your backhand or your least favorite shot say this out loud, "I can't believe I missed my favorite shot!" Say it loud enough for your opponents to hear. They are going to think you actually like your backhand and will hesitate to hit there again. They will probably hit fewer balls to your backhand which is what you want!

291 Ask Questions

Tony Robbins once said, "The quality of your life is determined by the quality of the questions you ask yourself." If you're not playing well, do you complain to your partner about your bad day? Do you say things like, "I can't believe how many times I've missed today. Why do I keep missing that shot? Why am I so bad today?" All of those questions give you negative and unproductive answers that make you lose faster. Instead, ask better questions like, "Where are their weaknesses? How high do they like the ball when they hit it hard?" Keep asking questions that help you find ways to exploit their weaknesses or make them uncomfortable. Ask your partner if they want to play two-back and lob more. Play I-formation when you are serving. Keep trying different things. Leave the complaints for another day and keep asking what can be done.

292 The Art of the Comeback

You are losing 6-4, 3-0, and on the changeover you and your partner start making comeback plans. First thing, remember the word: comeback. Now split the word, come back, specifically on the return side. Both players stay at the baseline on both the first and second serves. You benefit several ways when playing two-back. The net player doesn't have as large of a gap between you compared to when you are one up and one back. The net player has the middle to hit into, but you and your partner have more time to react to the volley. You also feel more like a team because you are together and you can still rush the net. In fact, it's very effective on a second serve with both players moving in together to look like a tidal wave approaching the server. Giving a different look to your opponents makes them think differently. You can also lob more to slow down the speed of the match. The longer you are on the court, the greater chance you have to make your comeback. Do as many different things to break their rhythm and your comeback will be an epic story!

293 Ready Position Grip

Should you have a forehand or backhand grip in the ready position? There isn't an absolute answer to this. Here's what I believe will help you. Because you have less time to hit your backhand, you should start with the backhand grip. You have more time to rotate your hand into the forehand grip as you turn your shoulders. You can turn your racket with your non-dominant hand while you rotate to find your grip. Your hand is also on the bigger space of the grip on a forehand which is much easier to feel. Some professionals have their non-dominant hand on the backhand and their dominant hand on the forehand. As I mentioned previously, there's no correct way. Try both and pick what suits you.

Here's a bonus tip. When your partner is serving and you are up at the net, look at the returner's grip. Oftentimes if they are holding a forehand grip, they prefer or are wanting to hit a forehand. Once you see their grips and tendencies, share that info with your partner.

294 Foot-Fault!

You noticed your opponent just made a foot-fault. You see on the next point that they foot-faulted again. What should you say and when do you say it? On the next changeover politely say this, "Hey! Not sure if you know, but I noticed that you keep foot-faulting. Just letting you know." That's all you should say. They will be aware that you are watching the next game he serves. If it continues, then on the next changeover politely say, "Don't want to make a big deal but you're still foot-faulting." Now get ready for some potential attitude from them. If they do it again, you have two options. You could just let it go, or the next game you serve, walk up to the middle of no-man's-land and serve from there. After your opponents lose their minds, just say, "If you're going to foot fault we will too!" That should take care of their foot faults!

295 From Where You Are

Your opponent hits a ball close to you at the baseline and it lands out. Typically the opponent farthest away from the shot asks, "Are you sure?" They might even say a few other snippy things. Here's the best way to handle your irrational opponents. Look directly at the main complainer and politely say, "From where you are I'm sure it looks like it's in. But I am right here and I can see it's definitely out." With this statement you are validating their feelings but also telling them that you are correct with your call and the ball is out. This should end the discussion.

296 Handling Heavy Topspin

Heavy topspin is a difficult skill for many players. The best way to volley a groundstroke with heavy topspin is to tighten your grip on contact. The feeling of contact with heavy topspin is like catching a medicine ball. It feels like your racket is getting pulled downward. Keep your wrist firm and try to keep your racket steady after contact. Like any difficult shot you face, hang tough and play a neutral shot. The pressure goes back to your opponents after you return it. Oftentimes they will hit the next shot harder and make an error.

297 Feedback

After practice, I was talking with Darlene about receiving feedback in the corporate world and the comparison to feedback in athletics. She mentioned that when receiving feedback, most people want to hear what they did well and not necessarily about what they did wrong. I believe feedback is good especially if you learn from it. Players often ask me what they did wrong when they missed. I like to ask them, "Do you know what you did right?" I will tell them what they did wrong, but the more important thing is to focus on what they want out of the shot rather than trying to prevent the same mistake. You get what you think about so think about executing the shot to your target the way you want.

298 Remember That Match...

C'mon, tell me about that comeback! You've most likely had an amazing comeback in your tennis career. It doesn't have to be as dramatic as a 0-6,0-5, Love-40, comeback victory. You could have just been down a match point or had a Love-40 game and comeback to win. What you should always remember in your matches is that you can do it again. Even if the task seems daunting, remember there's no clock in tennis. You have all day and all night to make your comeback. Tell yourself it's possible because like Kevin Garnett said, "Anything is possible!"

T.E.A.M.

Do you know what "T.E.A.M." stands for? Together Everyone Achieves More. You and your doubles partner are a team. Between points, connect with a high five, fist pump, clang your rackets together or just talk for a few seconds. You can blow off steam, pump each other up and strategize before the next point. When the game is over, walk to your benches together. If you're up at the net, wait for your partner or even walk halfway back and meet them then walk together to your bench. If you split sets and one of you needs a bathroom break, walk together to the bathroom. Usually the team that is winning connects whereas the team that's losing gets quiet and walks by themselves. When you connect you pull together. When you stay together between points, you can also come back to win faster.

300 Your Patience Caps

Strong teams wear their patience caps. After winning the first set in convincing fashion, 6-1, your partner starts serving to begin the second set. Your opponents choose to start two-back at the baseline and it starts. They start lobbing their return of serves. They lob the second and sometimes the third shot in the rallies. What they are trying to do is slow down your momentum. They are also saying that they can't beat you and are hoping that you lose to them. They hope you get frustrated with the slow pace and slow balls they are giving you. When this happens, look at your partner and tug on the front of your cap or visor, and remind your partner, "We are now wearing our patience caps." This will tell both of you to stay patient because all your opponents are doing is admitting they don't have the game to beat you. Be patient and show them you can beat them no matter what style they try to play.

301 The Dreaded Losing Streak

When you compete for several years, the dreaded losing streak is bound to happen. It might be 3, 4, 5, or worse. My worst was 7! The problem itself is when something bad happens and you feel a wave of more problems happening.

One mistake, then another, and another, and you feel like you can't win a single point. When you look back on your losing streak, you will probably find certain things were totally out of your control. For instance, during one of my losses, my partner missed an overhead on match point in the third set tiebreaker. To give yourself a break and to forget your previous losses, consider that you have also enjoyed a winning streak! If you would have won just your third match after losing the first two matches, you wouldn't have lost three in a row and then you wouldn't have had a losing streak. We often dwell on the last match too much. When you were on your winning streak, you probably felt like you would never lose a match. You enjoyed the benefits of certain key points going your way. Sometimes, getting over a losing streak can help you win more often. You will remember the bad feeling of losing, which keeps your focus when you are ahead in your matches. It all goes back to executing one point at a time rather than focusing on results. When you win or lose a point, your emotions stay neutral and you compete point after point.

302 Break the Rules

I can usually spot the players who rarely got in trouble as kids. They are very measured with their strokes and sometimes overly cautious. They also concentrate a bit too much on using correct technique, especially when they have to handle a difficult shot. When I encounter a player like this, I encourage them to let a few shots rip, get out of their cautious mindset, and misbehave a little. The biggest mistake in being too cautious is that you get tight on your strokes in an effort to be correct and follow all of the "rules." Try pushing past being too cautious in practice when you are winning. It's just practice so you can afford to go after a few. After a while, you will feel more relaxed by playing freely. So go ahead, break the rules and see what happens when you play freely!

303 Snap Your Wrist?

A major misconception about the serve is that you should snap your wrist. If you snap or even bend your wrist, your racket is moving downward and the weight of your racket causes stress on your wrist and forearm. What actually occurs is called pronation which is the turning over of your forearm. If you push your thumb downward as you are swinging through, you will see your forearm turn. Pronation also occurs after you throw a ball. That's why you might have heard it's good to throw a baseball or football to improve your serve. It's also important to swing loosely rather than thinking about how your arm is moving.

304 Roll Your Wrist?

Another major misconception is that you should roll your wrist over on your forehand to create topspin. Try bouncing a ball then rolling your wrist over the ball. The ball might have topspin, but it will land about a foot in front of you. A closed racket face brushing upwards creates lift and rotation a.k.a. topspin. Your forearm moves up with your elbow in a motion very similar to a windshield wiper. You can also push your racket from your right pocket and after you hit up on the ball, finish by your left shoulder. You will see your wrist move together with your forearm.

305 Stop and Hit?

You've heard it from teaching pros, parents, and even your partners. Stop and hit. However, you shouldn't completely stop to hit any shot. What "stop and hit" implies is that you should slow down and get your body under control. When you are hitting your groundstrokes, you want to drop below the ball by bending your knees. Try running, then come to a complete stop, then swing. Now try running to the ball and slow down naturally. You will realize that you don't totally stop. Just slow down and you'll be fine. Remember after you make your shot, you need to *move* into position for your opponent's next shot. Slow down and keep your balance.

Slow Then Slower

You're at the baseline and your opponent drives a strong shot towards you. You play a neutral ball back to them. They hit the next shot towards you again and you are tempted to drive a hard shot back at them. Remember, you lose control when you hit with power. Try this and see if you can force an error from your opponent. Hit your return back slower than you received it, then on the very next shot, hit it even slower. Your opponent will usually get frustrated and over hit the next shot. When you hit slowly, you are testing your opponent's patience while also hitting with a very high percentage. After playing defense on your opponent's hard shot you show great poise and confidence by hitting slowly.

High is Aggressive, Low is Safe

The biggest mistake besides lack of movement at the net, is being too aggressive with your volleys. If you are moving into the net with balance and the ball is above net height on contact, you can be aggressive. If your contact point is below the net and you are staying low, you should play a safe and high-percentage volley. Remember you don't have to make a winner with your volleys. Your chances of winning go up tremendously after making just one volley.

Be Wary of B-Level Advice

The B-level player knows just enough to be dangerous. They have had success moving up from the C-level and recently enjoyed some success in the B-level. They might know some instructive advice, but often misinterpret the root of the problem. If you're a B-level or even A-level player, remember to stay humble as it's a big tennis world. A good friend of mine was on the tour back in the late 80s. He was once ranked as high as #300 in the world. He told me he played a player ranked #1100 but lost terribly, 6-2, 6-1. He said the #1100 player was amazing. Funnily enough, none of us have ever heard about the #1100 ranked player. It's a huge tennis world with many great players. Stay humble and keep your mind open to keep getting better.

309 Rehab and Prehab

At the time of this writing, MK and Mike are about to have knee surgeries. Both players are "prehabbing." Prehab is building up the area around your injury with different exercises. Before my senior year in college, I had my right knee operated on in June, and my left knee done the first week of August. Because of my amazing mother, I was able to get through the long, painful, and frustrating summer. There's a large mental battle when coming back from a surgery or injury. The best advice is to be patient while giving your body time to heal. Your focus should be taking each day as it's own individual battle. This includes days when you are supposed to rest. You will be back on the courts when your body is ready. The last thing you want to do is rush your return and have a set back. If you don't want surgery or an injury, then make sure you do the off-court work like stretching, yoga, pilates, foam rolling, icing, and eating well. These are all little pieces of the puzzle which will help your on court performance tremendously.

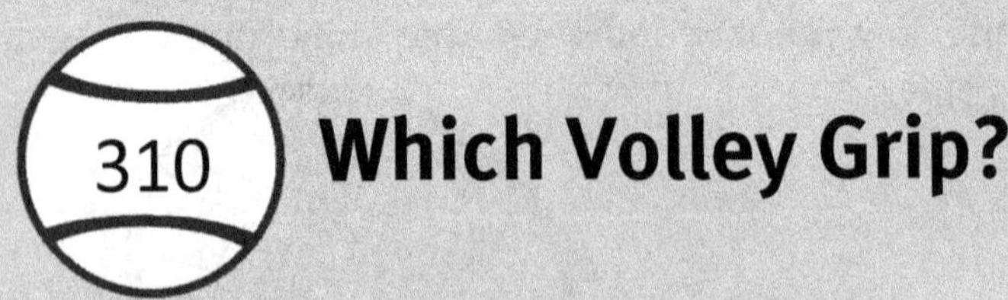

310 Which Volley Grip?

Hall of Famer, John McEnroe, was once asked which grip he used on his volleys. John's response was, "How high is the ball?" Typically, you should use a continental grip so you can volley both forehands and backhands without taking the time to change your grip. What McEnroe was alluding to is that if the ball is high, you can use an Eastern grip. This allows you to be more aggressive on the high volley. If you want a safe volley that also allows you to put some underspin on your volley, use the continental grip. If you're at the baseline and you can tell the net player is using a forehand grip, hit directly at them or towards their backhand to force the error or make them uncomfortable!

311 Why Did You Miss?

When I ask players why they missed their shot, they usually reference something they did wrong with their stroke. It could be a technical mistake but usually it is a tactical mistake. Technical refers to your stroke mechanics or fundamentals whereas tactical relies on your plan or strategy. Rick rushed the net towards Lindsay at the baseline. Lindsay then missed her down-the-line passing shot. When I asked Lindsay why she missed, she referenced her swing. It was partially a stroke error. I then asked her if she was trying to make her shot or hit a winner and she said she was trying to hit a winner past Rick in the alley. After she hit her winner, she told me she was just trying to hit the opening instead of winning the point. Remember you can't control the ending result of the point. Focus first on making your shot.

312 No-Man's-Land is Good

Yep! There is a time when it's good to be in no-man's-land. During a practice, Gosia hit a deep lob that pushed Missy deep behind the baseline. Missy returned Gosia's lob with a high lob that pushed Gosia back behind her baseline. Now here's where no-man's-land is good. When you hit a lob, the most likely shot to return it is another lob. You don't want to get pushed behind your baseline, especially after you pushed your opponent back. When you lob, move into no-man's-land. Instead of letting your opponent's lob bounce high and push you backwards, block or volley their lob out of the air. This keeps you on the offensive and takes time away from your opponent. After you take the lob out of the air, you should move to the service line to take even more time away from your opponents.

313 Be Careful of Winning

You've won so frequently in the last month that you feel invincible. Enjoy that feeling because you usually feel like crap when you lose. Feeling bad means you are a true competitor. When you win frequently in a short span of time, it's easy to become overconfident which can lead to bad habits. Your focus isn't the same and you feel like winning just happens. It's gratifying to think about your winning record but playing like you lost your last match might be a better way to approach your next match. You want to be laser focused about executing your shots and staying in the moment rather than thinking about victory. Winning is great for your confidence, but to compete like this current match is all that matters is a better mindset than playing with an overconfident attitude.

314 Less is More

Less is more is about the way you should volley. You should be aggressive with your feet and use your hands for control and placement of your shot. Try deflecting or redirecting the ball as softly as possible. You can put some pop or really stick your volley at times, yet if you think about placement and touch, less actually will be more when you volley.

315 What Causes No-Man's-Land?

Most mistakes are caused by poor judgment which is a mental mistake. Getting stuck in no-man's-land is both a physical and a mental mistake. I've never been big on excuses, but here's where you can blame your opponent for your mistake. When your opponent has a weak and slow second serve, it doesn't make sense to stand behind the baseline. You should step up into no-man's-land to return their serve. This is easier than having to run from the baseline, scrambling to get to the short serve. After you return, you need to go to at least the service line, or even back behind the baseline. Decide between being on offense or going to play defense. There's nothing worse than being non-committal and staying in no-man's-land. Either get back or go!

316 Freeze Tag

Do you remember that game you played on the playground when you were a kid? Hit your volleys like you are playing freeze tag. A major mistake on volleys is to swing and hit. When you volley, squeeze and freeze your hand as you make contact. In freeze-tag, you stop when you are touched. In the case of tennis, freeze when you touch the ball. When you freeze your hand, you will stop any swinging motion. Literally reach your hand forward to get your racket out in front of you, then freeze on contact. Keep your feet pumping through your volley as well.

317 Play Tennis Poker

If you think about the toughest opponents you've ever faced, they likely have a calm, confident, and even stoic demeanor while competing. You can rarely tell if they are up or down mentally. Too many players get caught up in yelling and excessive fist pumping early in their matches, but become mopey when losing. These highs and lows are energy drainers. Remember to be mentally tough so you don't become too high or too low and continue to compete point after point. Give yourself a goal for your next match that you are going to have a poker face so your opponent won't know what you're thinking.

318 Too Many Choices

In practice, Eric was moving in on a short and easy ball until he did what all of us have done... he missed. He then looked at me and said, "I had too many choices." Several minutes later the same thing happened to Jed. Both Eric and Jed are excellent players, but why did they miss easy shots when they had so many choices to win the point? Remember to keep your thoughts simple on all shots. If you asked a professional what they think when they get an easy ball, they would tell you they maintain tunnel vision to the target. You should create a picture in your mind of your shot going *in*. You don't know if your shot will be a winner, so if it does come back, don't worry because you will probably receive another easy ball. When that happens, keep tunnel vision and execute!

319 Into the Wind

There's nothing more frustrating than playing tennis on a windy day even if the temperatures are warm. When you lob in the wind, lob towards the middle so you have more room for your lob to land in. When you are at the net and receive a lob in the wind, step back and let the lob bounce in front of you instead of trying to deal with the ball being pushed down. Letting the ball bounce gives you more time to make the shot. Above all else just be patient. Today the wind was 25 mph! Jess, Laura, MK, Marjorie and Alyssa had a patience testing lesson today but know how to deal with the wind.

320 What Would Happen If...

You love playing the baseline and your groundstrokes are great to set up your net partner. Here's a challenge and opportunity for you. During the next practice match you play, move into the service box with every short ball or second serve you receive. In doing this, you might get passed, have to volley, or hit an overhead. Your opponents could miss in the net, hit the ball over the baseline or hit it out over the sidelines. Your opponents will feel pressure after you constantly move into the service box to attack them. You might notice that the majority of times when you attack, you win the point. Your strong groundstrokes make it difficult for your opponents to pass you and you also receive easy volleys because you're forcing weak replies from your opponents. Try it, be bold, and go!

321 Your Poaching Path

One of the things I always point out to players after drill sessions is the poaching path. On clay courts, you can see your footprints, your skids, and your sliding patterns. If your footprints go sideways, or lateral, you won't poach well. You want your path to go on a diagonal pattern. Diagonal movement will help you receive a higher volley and more angles to volley into. You can also think, "Straight to the ball," which will make you move in the right direction. Keep moving forward and be a great volleyer like Tina, Diedre, Sheila, MK and Allie!

322 We're All Guilty

While working on approach shots followed by closing out the point with a volley, my player, Mike, said something that's true for all players: "We're all guilty of it!" Mike was referring to missing easy shots. When players see an easy shot they tend to get lazy with their feet. Players lose their focus because they assume they've already won the point. That's why it is so crucial, especially when you are on defense, that you get the ball back in anyway you can. There's always the possibility that your opponent will get lazy, lose focus, and totally blow it! Keep your focus on a proactive fundamental and execute. You'll get the applause and high-five *after* you hit your winner!

323 Strings and Shoes

How often should you restring your racket? There's a belief that the number of times you play per week is the number of times you should restring per year. However a more accurate way to determine is the number of *hours* spent on court during a week. You could play three times a week for an hour, or you could play once a week for three hours. Either way, you are logging the same amount of court time per week. Most players restring about three or four times a year. I recommend starting with March, then again in June, then again in September. If you play through the winter, restring once more in December. When you restring, also look at the bottom of your shoes. People forget how fast shoes wear out because the outside is still clean. The cushion in your shoes will wear down, so make sure to invest in new shoes which is cheaper than a foot injury. Another way to get a little more life in your game is to experiment with different strings and string gauges. You might find you get a better feel with different strings or a thinner gauge. Most importantly, *never* leave your racket in your car or garage! The extreme temperatures in your garage will make them lifeless and feel dead. Taking care of your rackets and shoes are just as important as your forehands and backhands.

324 Finding Rhythm

Clint and Steve are just beginning their careers as a doubles team. They both have good strokes but don't have many seasons under their belts yet. Steve mentioned that during a match when he misses, he looks forward to fixing his mistake on the next point. We as players have this conversation in our heads saying, "I'm going to make the next one." That's a good thought, but it can be frustrating because you can't change that you lost the last point. Say you missed a backhand return. You look forward to the next return so you can make your backhand and correct your previous mistake. The server then serves to your forehand

and it might be a few more minutes before you get another backhand. All you want to do is get another backhand and find your rhythm. Finding rhythm in a match takes time, but sometimes you might never get your rhythm on a particularly bad day. You should just compete one point at a time and stop trying to fix previous mistakes. Forget your errors and keep analyzing what your opponents are doing. This is more helpful so you don't continue beating yourself up mentally.

325 Action Beats Reaction

Do you want to feel bold or do you want to feel afraid in a match? All players should want to feel bold. Before each point, remember action beats reaction. Your action could be stepping to the side so you can return a forehand. You step as they toss so the opposing net player is wary of your forehand drive. You could be the returner's partner and after your partner returns crosscourt, you squeeze the middle and dare the baseliner to hit down-the-line from behind their baseline. After a successful poach, you fake before your partner's serve bounces in. All of these moves make your opponent think about your movement before they hit. When you hit you want to feel comfortable and when you move before they hit, they feel uncomfortable. Your action forces a reaction and you will be in control of the point.

326 Pump It Up!

When players are first learning topspin, they often get afraid they will hit the ball out because they are swinging upwards. When you see the ball rotate towards your opponent's side of the court, the force of the spin is pushing downwards. When you accelerate your racket upwards and generate more spin, the ball actually pushes faster, downward into the court. As a bonus, the ball will quickly jump up off of the court and your opponent has to deal with a higher bouncing ball. Trust your topspin will stay in. Remember to accelerate up!

327 It's Called a "Christy!"

"Doc" Wayne Christy was a legendary baseball coach and tennis player at Westminster College. He was also my third grade Sunday school teacher. We would often start Sunday school with conversations about the Titan athletic performances from the previous day. After a few minutes he would say, "Now Robbie, we need to focus on today's lesson." I can still see him turn the pages of his Bible with his left hand and hear the pages crinkle. Doc Christy had an amazing knack for hitting net cord shots. Usually they went over the net and he won the point. He did it so often that it became known as "hitting a Christy." When your opponent's shot hits the net and bounces on your side of the court, remember to tell yourself to slow down! Most athletes will panic and speed up their shot which creates a lack of control and inevitably miss the shot. The net slows down your opponent's shot which gives you more time to hit your shot. Sometimes the ball will drop straight down and that's just bad luck. Usually the ball pops up which will give you time to collect yourself briefly and then you can make your shot.

328 Of All the Athletes I've Ever Coached...

In my junior year of college, we were in the van on the way home from an away match. Coach Bob Pearson went around calling out every player's last name followed by a brief compliment. In the direction he was going. I could tell I was going to be last to receive one of his thoughtful and well deserved compliments. Finally I heard "Carver! Of all the athletes I've ever coached..., " then an interminable silence. I was preparing for the most amazing compliment, and then he said, "Of all the athletes I've ever coached, you're one of them!" The entire van, including myself, laughed like crazy! Another thing Coach Pearson would say to us during practice and our matches was, "Bad luck!" We didn't want to hear it because we had just lost a point, but the wisdom said so much. Bad luck is part of sports and there's nothing you can do about it. What you can do is move on and go after the next point. Thanks

Coach Pearson! I've told that story many times and I am the lucky one to be one of the athletes you coached!

High to the Backhand

You are serving to the deuce side and your opponent lobs over your partner. You are now running to get the lob bouncing high to your backhand. Not a very comfortable shot, is it? Almost every player would prefer to receive a ball at waist height, opposed to shoulder level or even higher. If that's the case, then why do we drive most shots? It's not only the shots that we want to hit that are most effective, but the kind of shots that your opponents don't like to receive. Start out by hitting high lobs to their backhands. If your opponent has a strong forehand drive, hit a slow looper to see if it breaks their rhythm. The high bounce is uncomfortable for most players especially on the backhand side.

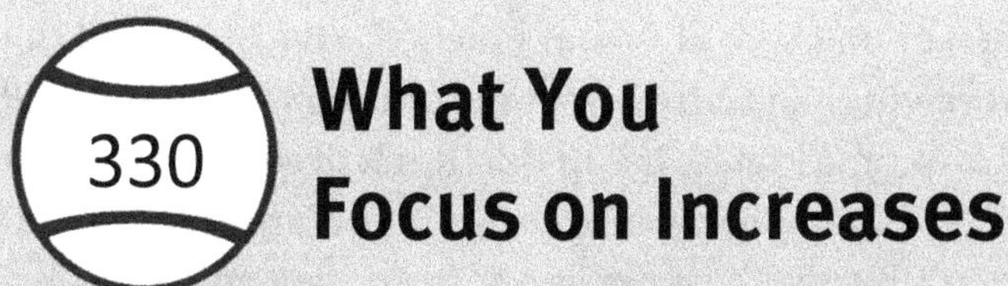

What You Focus on Increases

You just hit your fourth groundstroke in a row into the net. You look at your partner and say, "That's the fourth time in a row that I've hit the net!" During the next two games you hit three more into the net. On the change-over you tell your partner, "If I don't stop hitting the net, we have no chance." A colorful display of profanity ensues after your next three net errors. If I was coaching you and just told you to try to hit it over the net, you might call me Captain Obvious. That poor advice and your comments about your poor performance just solidify your thoughts about hitting the net and make it more of a reality. A better way to compete is to tell yourself what you *want,* rather than to focus on your errors. My better advice to you would be to aim eight feet higher, or hit towards their hats. Take your focus off of your errors and concentrate on lifting the ball and putting it in play!

331 Challenges Make You Better

Do you have a teammate or friend that hits a shot that you struggle returning? Or is there a shot you don't hit very well? Every player, including professionals, has a certain shot they hate returning. So what do you do with a shot you can't seem to handle? Ask your teammate to hit a dozen of that shot at you in practice. You still might not like receiving it, but through time and repetition you will get more comfortable. If you don't practice it, it will never improve. Now what about the shot you are trying to hit but don't hit well? For instance, you want to improve a slice serve with the continental grip. Putting in the time and repetition will help you get more comfortable and you should see improvement. My dad once told me, "Change is scary but that's what makes life exciting. Never be afraid of a challenge!" Look at a challenging shot as a fun way to improve.

332 Lift, Loop, Lob

You're on the run moving off of the court to return your opponent's wicked angle. You see a tiny opening down-the-line and want to hit an amazing winner like the one you saw on TV. When you're on the run, think lift, loop, or lob. You need to lift to first clear the net. Secondly, you want your shot to be hit with a loop or higher arc. The loop can also be a lob if you're on defense and need recovery time. When you lob, your partner also has time to get back inside the court in case your opponent hits an overhead. If you are losing and you lift, loop, and lob, you will put more balls in play and while also slowing down the speed of the match. Hopefully you can break your opponent's rhythm and make a comeback.

333 Attack!

Attack with your feet! When you are at the net and you receive a high ball, you have a great opportunity to win the point with a strong volley. Too often players will take a big swing, over hit, and miss the easy ball. Rather than swinging, attack with your feet. You will create momentum for your volley and get yourself closer to the net. When you get close to the net, you have more angles to hit into. Another benefit is that you are taking time away from your opponents. Attacking with your feet is smart not only on high balls, but all volleys.

Tennis and Orchestra

"Hey Coach Rob, tennis has helped my orchestra!" Charlotte yelled to me at the beginning of her practice. I quickly looked at her sister Maddie to see if they were playing a joke on me. When I asked how tennis has helped her orchestra, she explained, "Tennis is all about timing and rhythm just like orchestra!" My thoughts went immediately to one of my best mentors, Hall of Fame Band Director, Gene Inglis. It might not be the same as actually taking part in an orchestra, but it's helpful to listen to your favorite music or song before a match. It can get you in a good mindset before your game and calm your nerves. To improve your timing and rhythm say "bounce, hit" when the ball bounces and when you hit your shot.

335 You Have a Mantra?

After Sarah closed out a point with a volley she looked at me and said, "I have a new mantra. 'Take away their time!'" Getting to your shot earlier, moving to net position, and taking balls out of the air all take time away from your opponent. This is a great strategy from Sarah. So what is your mantra? I challenge you to come up with a new mantra every season or every month.

Here are some examples:

I return and close in on second serves.
I poach early and often.
I out move everyone on the court.

Make sure you keep your mantras proactive. Things like, "I never miss," or "I never double fault," sound like they are good mantras, but trying to prevent yourself from doing certain things actually puts more pressure on yourself. Keep your mantras proactive and you will have a more expansive and improving mindset.

336 Failure or Growth Moment?

In practice with junior players, I will often challenge them to aim for targets. Too often, when one player misses the target, another player says, "You failed!" I always respond by saying, "He didn't fail at all. He just missed. You only fail when you give up!" All players will have a bad match in which they played poorly, or played well but missed in a crucial moment. Sometimes players just choke! It's a terrible feeling and you may feel like you failed but whatever happens you must take it as a growth moment. In all competitions, you either win or you learn. However, you should make it a goal to also learn when you win. Everytime I play a match, something new is revealed to me about tennis. Yes, everytime! It's amazing what you can learn when you keep an open mind. Make it your goal to be a continual learner with your game and the things you discover about yourself and your opponents.

337 Fathers and Sons

There's nothing better than being a son whose dad is good at tennis. I owe a lot of my development to my father. When I was 13, I started hitting against a wall while my dad was on the next court playing singles. Then I got the tennis bug where you want to hit the ball for hours and hours. My dad was very patient with my development. He gave up hundreds of afternoons hitting and playing matches against me. The court time we shared is time I will always treasure.

In the last few years, I've enjoyed watching several junior boys develop into very strong players. Their dads are also students of mine. The development and improvement of the boys has been very gratifying for me as well as their dads. There will be a day when the boys will be better than their dads. When that day comes men, relish in the fact that you contributed, not only in your financial investment, but emotionally as well. Corey and BA, HD and Harrison, Jake, Nico and Pierre, Jason and Jake...enjoy the court time together. It's a gift for fathers and sons. It's also a gift for moms and daughters.

338 Releasing the Valve

I read somewhere that anger is only one letter away from danger. Anger is normal, especially during competition. The danger comes when you show your opponent your anger. They will feed off of your negative actions because they know you are frustrated and will most likely make you hit the exact shot that you just missed. A good way to deal with your anger is what I call "releasing the valve." Rather than letting your frustration build to its boiling point, tell your partner your frustration. It's kind of like venting to a friend or your spouse. You always feel better when you let it out. I don't care when you share your feelings with your partner, or if your language becomes a little colorful or even obscene. Whatever your feelings are, just let them out. When your rant is over agree to move on for the better. Remember to approach the game one point at a time and release the valve if you must.

339 The Four Deadliest Words in Tennis

Tennis is a game filled with mistakes and can be incredibly frustrating at times. Letting a few obscene words fly after missing can be therapeutic but also detrimental for your game. However, the four deadliest words in tennis are: can't, quit, tired, and sorry. When verbalized, these words are self-esteem killers that will also fire up your opponents after they hear how negative and down you are. Like the previous tip explained about releasing the valve, dropping a more colorful word is okay and understandable. Move on to the next point after you miss your shot.

340 Never, Ever Say Sorry!

What's wrong with apologizing to your teammate when you miss? Your partner should know that you didn't mean to miss and you were trying to make the correct play. You felt bad after your first error. Did you feel twice as bad when you made the second error? You probably did! By verbalizing your sad feelings and regrets, you are dragging both yourself and your partner down. Everyone makes mistakes and there's a possibility your opponent will miss on the very next point. Remember the right plays you've made and forget what you didn't execute.

Success Leaves Clues

Think about your last match. What shots did your deuce side opponent hit well? What about the ad side player? Who was the better volleyer? Who served better? Which directions did they serve more often? All of these questions should be discussed between you and your partner as the match progresses. Just like your weapons that win points, your opponents have their own strengths. It's your job to remember their successful patterns so you can adjust your strategy accordingly. Make note of what worked for you and your partner throughout your successful points. The team that wins is often the team that adjusts to the successful patterns and shots of their opponents. Success leaves clues if you're able to look for them.

342 First Strike Tennis

After a recent match, Mary told me that she didn't feel like a good doubles player because her groundstrokes are stronger than her volleys. As much as volleys are important in doubles, you can still be an effective partner if they aren't your strength. Picture yourself hitting a strong return-of-serve that the server weakly returns in the middle of the court. What do you think your partner at the net will do? They have an opportunity to knock off a volley winner. They had an easy ball because you made the server hit a weak reply. Your baseline game can run your opponents off of the court with angles, and when you lob the opposing net player you are also running your opponents. When they run they are weaker and your partner can then control the point with their volleys. If you don't volley well, concentrate on hitting smart and effective groundstrokes to set up your partner at the net.

343 Finding Your Serving Rhythm

During practice, Adam, Sam, Joshua, and Zachary were practicing their serves. There are many moving parts to the serve. Unfortunately, thinking about all of the moving parts makes the serve even more difficult. If you asked a touring professional what they thought about before hitting their serve, they would probably tell you which direction they intended to hit. Executing any shot in tennis is more of a feeling than box checking your technique. What I mean by that is to analyze your technique as you are hitting. You don't have time to process all of the things that happen during any stroke. When developing your serving rhythm, you can benefit from telling yourself something proactive before you start your serving motion like, "Down up and hit; 1, 2, and 3." Once you have your rhythm picture where you want your serve to land and let it rip!

344 Never Say Second Serve

I always enjoy gaining more wisdom from students. One of my players, Liz, told me that she never announces the second serve before she hits it. She said it negatively reinforces to herself that she missed her first serve. I really like that mindset. There's nowhere in the rules that says you have to announce your second serve to your opponent. It's a given that if they miss their first serve they will make a second. If you are the returner and they say, "Second serve," this is your indicator that a potentially weaker serve is coming your way. This is your opportunity to return the serve and make the next shot difficult for the server. Pre-plan where you want your return to go so that you have tunnel vision to your target.

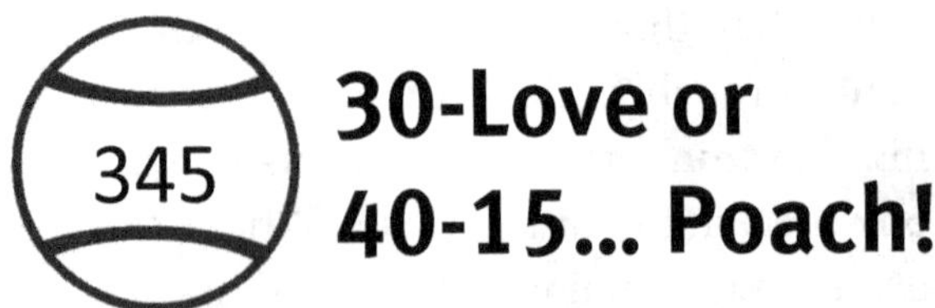

30-Love or 40-15... Poach!

You are the server's partner at the net and winning 30-Love, or even better, winning 40-15. If you were the returner, would you be bold and hit down-the-line or hit high-percentage crosscourt? You would probably play smart and hit high-percentage crosscourt. Now you are at the net and your partner serves. You should plan to move towards the middle and poach. If the returner hits a sharp angle that you can't reach, your partner can run and return it. If the returner happens to hit a winner down-the-line you are still winning. Odds are your opponents won't hit 2 winners in a row on the return of serve. If they do, you are still tied. When you are winning, look for their high percentage return and be bold.

Read Their Rackets

Would you open or close your racket face if you are going to lob? What about driving a groundstroke? When you lob your racket face is open. When you drive a groundstroke with topspin the racket face is closed. Most of you already know that, so why are you surprised when you rush the net and you don't react when they lob? If you watch your opponent's racket face, rather than the ball, you will see what type of shot they are about to hit. Your opponents will usually lean back when they lob and then lean into their groundstroke drives. Being aware of this helps you prepare for their shot.

347 Miss in The Middle

You might think this means to aim through the middle of the court. Aiming through the middle of the court is smart, however, there are times when you should hit down-the-line. When you hit down-the-line you should aim for the middle of the alley. A common mistake is to miss wide because you aimed for the doubles sideline. The alley is only 4 ½ feet wide, so when you aim for the middle of the alley, you are giving yourself over two feet of space, should you miss the middle of the alley.

348 Your Fourth Option

When you win the racket toss before the match, did you know that you have four options? You can choose to serve, receive, pick a side, or defer the choice to your opponents. Many players aren't aware that they can defer to their opponents. Why defer? Let's say you defer and your opponents choose to serve. You get to choose the side you prefer to start on. If they choose the court side first, you can then pick between serve or return. There's no real advantage in deferring but it does put your opponents on notice that you have a plan. Try it next time you win the toss and see what type of reaction your opponents give you.

349 The ABC's of Serving

You step up to the baseline to serve and wonder where you should aim. Your coach said serving to their backhand is smart, but you're unsure if your opponent will run around their backhand and hit a forehand. You can never know exactly what your opponent will do. You also don't know if you will win the point. When you step up to the line, make your focus tunnel vision to your target. Keep your thoughts simple then hit with belief that you will make your shot. Just remember your ABCs to maintain your focus.

> A = serving towards the *Alley* also known as serving out wide
> B = serving towards your opponent's *Body* which is the middle of the box
> C = serving towards the *Center* or serving towards the T

When you practice your serve, vary where you aim. Too often players will just practice serving towards their favorite location in hopes of hitting aces during the match. Hitting to different spots keeps your opponent off balance.

350 Give Me Fuel, Give Me Fire...

If you're a Metallica fan you are probably getting fired up thinking about the song "Fuel." Just remember however that you don't want to fuel your opponent's fire. A common mistake when hitting hard is that your opponent might like the pace you are sending them. For example, when you hit a hard approach shot and your opponent likes the pace, they will be ripping a passing shot back at you which will be difficult to volley. If you prefer to hit hard, remember to mix in a slower shot every few shots to break your opponent's rhythm. Remember the hard hitter you are facing might love the fuel you are providing.

351 Don't Be Afraid to Change

Have you ever seen *Rocky IV*? After beating Ivan Drago in Russia, Rocky addressed the crowd, "If I can change, then you can change, then maybe everyone can change!" Think of this in terms of tennis. Do you stand in the same spot in the service box when your partner is serving? Do you return serve from the same position because it's comfortable? That is okay, however it doesn't give you an advantage against your opponents. You need to change! When you change your positions your opponents usually change the patterns of their shots. Seeing you do something different forces them to think differently. If you feel uncomfortable in a new position, your opponents are also uncomfortable because they have to change the way they respond. Have the courage to change!

352 Eat Your Vegetables!

Remember when you were a kid and your Mom made you eat a particular vegetable that you didn't like? What did she say? "Because it's good for you!" Every player has a shot that they don't like to hit and will oftentimes run around their weaknesses so they only have to hit their strengths. In a match you certainly want to hit your strength as much as possible, but there will be times when you have to hit your weaker shot. If you never hit it, your weakness will always be a liability for you. Build up your weaknesses by hitting them in practice, just like eating your vegetables will help your body stay healthy!

The Swinging Volley

The swinging volley is hit just like a regular volley, but you are swinging at the ball like it's a groundstroke. It does require better timing, but can be a better option if you prefer swinging for shots rather than making a firm volley. The swinging volley can be played in place of any shot on offense, defense, or as a neutral shot. You want to swing upwards with topspin to create lift and give plenty of clearance over the net.

Stay in Your Position

We've all received a slow ball and we hit it too long. The same shot comes to you again and you hit it into the net. The frustrating part of these errors is that you received a relatively easy ball but lost the point. The most likely reason that you missed the shot is because you got out of your athletic position. If you picture anyone returning serve, you should see a balanced athletic position: knees bent, butt down, head up. Getting out of the athletic position too soon leads to many technical errors. You should sit when you hit and keep your head as still as possible. My friend, Greg, made this correction in my form as he told me that I stand up too soon leading me to miss many returns. Since he pointed that out, my returns have improved greatly. By staying in the athletic position as you hit, you will have better timing as well as good technique.

355 Predictable Patterns

Every player has a favorite shot or favorite place to hit certain shots. My challenge to you is to discover very early what kind of shot and where they like to hit it. Believe it or not you can find their preferences during warm-ups. Players hit their favorite shots first so pay attention to their first serve. Rarely will a player hit their least favorite shot first. During the first game the direction of their first shots will also tip you off to where they like to hit. Whenever you reach deuce for the first time, remember which direction they hit. The same is true when the score is ad-in or ad-out. We all have our "go to" shots and patterns. By the second set, you and your partner should have discussed which patterns you both saw. You will be able to predict them because you looked for their patterns.

356 Hit Your Second, First!

I spent a practice working on serves with up-and-coming juniors, Nate and Zach. After a few warm-ups, I told them to start practicing their second serves. They looked at me like I was crazy. Everyone wants to hit a booming, powerful first serve that wins points. But what happens when you miss that big first serve? How effective is your second serve? Unfortunately, many players hit a hard first serve followed by a slow, weak, second serve. There's a popular tennis phrase that goes, "You're only as good as your second serve." When you practice your second serve frequently, you build confidence. With that confidence in your second serve, you can be more relaxed as you hit your first. I recommend you hit with your second serve early in the match. Your opponent is looking for a hard first serve. Start building up your second serve so that you have confidence in it. You will be glad you spent the time building up your second serve as you see your overall service percentage go up!

357 Tell Your Partner

You are playing the deuce side and returning serve. The serve pulls you into the alley and you return down-the-line. Unfortunately, the opposing net player volleyed your shot between you and your partner. One way to prevent this is to tell your partner your intentions before the serve. For instance, you could tell your partner that if the serve pulls you into the alley, you will hit down-the-line so they will cover the middle. You could also tell your partner that you will lob if you receive a backhand. If they know you are going to lob, they can prepare to back up if your lob is short. When you communicate with your partner before the point begins, you two will be on the same page and aware of your opponents next possible shots.

358 Hanging Tough

Your opponents just had five break points on your service game. You were down, 15-40, and battled back to deuce. Then they had three more break chances. Your partner made a few key poaches and you hit two big serves to help you hold serve. The ending of this point doesn't really matter, because the main takeaway is that you held serve. They had many chances and still didn't break your serve! It's common to feel like you are in trouble the next time you serve because they had chances, but consider how frustrated your opponents must feel after losing so many opportunities. During the next game you serve, your focus on the very first point should be very high as if the score is deuce. You won't let them reach 15-40 this time! You can take any situation and turn it as a positive if your mindset is to hang tough!

359 Two Cans and No Switching

I recently played on indoor courts with my good friend Greg. When I opened up two cans of balls, he said, "Hey Carver, why are you opening up two cans of balls?" I learned this tip from the late Arthur Ashe. In one of his books he said that when you play indoors, open up two cans of balls and don't switch sides. You are paying for valuable court time so make the most of it. When I practice or play for fun, I always open up two cans of balls to have more hitting time and less time retrieving balls. What is a few bucks to get more hitting time?

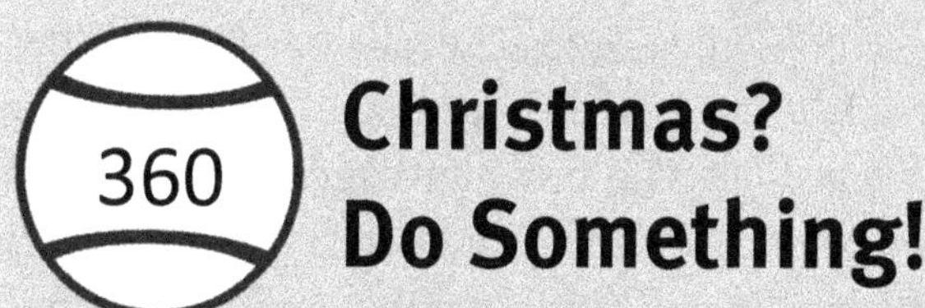

360 Christmas? Do Something!

Take Jocko Willink's advice, "You can take a day off, just not today!" Everyday is a day to do something. You can just spend fifteen minutes stretching if you don't want to leave your house. Take a long walk with your family and when you get to a hill or incline, walk backwards. Even better, put on your new warm-up outfit and go hit twenty-five serves and do ten minutes of footwork. These little sacrifices add up to build your mental toughness. When you are playing a hard match, think back on these moments and use them to pull through the harder plays.

When you look across the net, question whether your opponents have worked as hard as you. Remember when you didn't want to work out and you did anyway!

Dominate the Deuce Side

Your partner is serving and you are in the service box. The returner will usually hit their first return crosscourt. You can let your partner return it or you can be bold and poach. If you poach successfully, you will be winning. If you miss, you will still be sending a message to the returner that you control the middle of the court. When you control the middle, the returner has less space to hit into. When you show the deuce side returner that you are willing to poach, they will feel pressure to keep their return away from you. The potential threat of poaching will always be present in their mind. Additionally, if you fake when the ball lands in the service box, your opponent will return down-the-line right to you. See how many ways you can distract the returner with your movement. If you are right handed you will have a forehand volley in the middle of the court which also makes it easier to poach. If you're left handed you can still poach even with your backhand because most shots travel crosscourt.

362 Rain Day

How does a tennis player practice if they don't have access to an indoor court? My chiropractor, Dr. Sarah Wilkie, told me that constantly being on a hard court doesn't do any favors for our bodies. Hard courts don't have any give like a clay court. Rainy days are the perfect day to take care of your tennis body. Yoga or any form of an all body stretch is very beneficial. Yes men, you should do yoga! It can be uncomfortable at first, but if you do it on a consistent basis, you will reap major rewards. Flexibility, strength, coordination, and balance will all improve, according to Tony Horton, the creator of P90X. Foam rolling should be done on a daily basis. Check out my YouTube (Rob Carver Tennis) if you need a demonstration! Unfortunately we will all suffer from inflammation at some point. Ice is a wonder drug whether it's your shoulder, elbow, or knees. Icing is so much better than living out of a bottle. All of these off-court measures are pieces of the puzzle. Take care of your body off the court so you can perform better on the court!

363 One Fundamental

As with any new skill there's a learning curve. Too often, we as coaches give an overload of information. This can make our students feel overwhelmed to try to do many things correctly. This can also happen with accomplished players during a match. They will overthink and try to do many technical things correctly, while also trying to direct the ball away from the opponent. When you feel like you are doing this, just keep your attention on one fundamental. For instance, if you're right handed, when trying to get more spin on your serve, hit one o'clock on the ball. If you're trying to get more topspin out of a groundstroke, think about hitting the bottom of the ball. There are many good fundamentals that you should practice, but keep your thoughts on only one fundamental and you should execute your shots better.

364 What Does a Pro Think

Recently, Lourdes and Brittany were on defense hitting difficult shots. They were so deep in the court that it was nearly impossible for them to drive their groundstrokes. Their best play was to lob. Jen then asked a very important question: "What does a pro think when they are on defense?"

A touring pro will think about lobbing as well, but more importantly they will believe that their shot will always go in whether on offense or defense. You want to picture your shot going in everytime, in the exact fashion you want. When you picture your shot going in, it actually takes the pressure of winning off of you. Always keep your thoughts proactive and in your mind's eye, see it going in.

365 What Do You Want to Hear?

The question is about what you want to hear from yourself as you are playing your match. If you could have your thoughts and self-talk printed out for everyone to read, would people think you're a tough competitor or someone who was always berating themselves? On numerous occasions I have told players, "If I talked to you the way you talk to yourself you would never let me coach you again. Give yourself a break!" You are going to be bad on some days and others you are going to screw up royally. That's just the way tennis is sometimes. Start practicing talking to yourself as if you were coaching yourself. You shouldn't compound your error by speaking derogatory to yourself. What's done is done and you need to move on. Furthermore, you wouldn't dare speak to your partner in a negative way. The next time you catch yourself speaking like that to yourself, remember that no one should speak to your partner's partner like that!

366 The Most Important # in Tennis

Thanks Coach, you waited this long to tell us? Yep! I wanted to make sure you read the entire book! The most important number in tennis is 2. You have to win by a margin of 2 points to win a game. You have to win by a margin of 2 games to win a set. You have to win a tie-breaker by a margin of 2 points, as well. Rather than waiting until 30-All or deuce, lock in on the first point with your goal of winning 2 in a row. Keep playing every game as mini two-point games. You will get locked in to those strategies that work and then go back to back winning points. Before you even think about winning points, focus on making 2 shots in a row. Seventy-three percent of all rallies are won in four shots or less. By making just 2 shots per rally you are greatly increasing your chances of winning. What do you think if you have to hit three shots? Think about where your target is, just like you did when you made your first 2 shots. In your mind stick with making 2, then winning 2, and you will be winning back to back titles as well!

ACKNOWLEDGMENTS

To all my clients, thank you for your commitment to improving with the many enjoyable hours of effort, sweat, and laughter on the courts.

Thank you, Tom Gorman, for the wonderful forward and your kind words. I appreciate your trust in me to teach your daughters, as well as your friendship.

To my family, Heather, Ella, and Dean. You three are my all time favorite team!

To my parents, Tom and Betty Carver, for your unconditional love, encouragement, support, and wisdom.

Rick, Melanie, and Kody Carver, Naomi and Keith Williams, Abbey and Hunter Hays, Sandy and Nancy Boardman, Tom Ritchey, Wilson Door, Steve Gould, Graham Carter, Dar Huey, Patrick Shannon, David and Phillip Herrin.

My fur babies, Blanca, Shrek, Chloe, Logan, Nittany and Zoe. Thanks for all the hugs, wags, and never ending craziness, especially on rainy days.

Wilson Racket Sports: Jim Haneklau, Evan Garfinkel, Iain Pound

USPTA and USPTA GA Chapter

Sandestin Resort: Todd Hanson and David Brandt

Southern Tennis Academy: Steve Dixon

Truett McConnell University

Berry College

My Tennis Brothers: Dr. Adam Shafran, Adam Kework, Bryan Humphreys, Chris King, Chris Stroumpis, Darryl Laddin, Steve Brandt, Howard Sappington, Greg Dickson, Greg Caccia, John Hanna, Mike Dowse, Tom Warren, Chris Merrill, Steve Brandt, Nicholas Stroumpis, James Mullis, Tony Wright, Tracy Perry, Mike Byrne, Mark Byrne, Steve Christianson, Grant Novitz, Shane Phitides, Richard Lunney, Terry Michelitch, Ben White, William McClelland, Tim Kullick.

Coaches: Nell Carver, Tom Carver, Pam Wilson, Dwight Ellenburg, Terri Whitehurst, Rodney Fitzgerald, Todd Smyly, Bob Pearson, Jaleel Riaz

Mentors: Tom Daglis, Ken DeHart, Tom Gorman

Book Consultants: Roy Berger, Dar Huey

Editor: Ella C. Carver

YouTube Videographer: Dean Carver

And a special thanks to the team at Booklogix!

Last but not least, thank you Jesus for your grace… the most amazing gift!

ABOUT THE AUTHOR

Rob Carver is a certified USPTA Elite Professional and the owner of Rob Carver Tennis Inc. since 1992. He teaches approximately 160 students per week throughout Marietta and Roswell, GA, of ages ranging from 5 to 75 years old. Rob graduated from Berry College with a degree in Psychology. Rob played collegiate tennis at Truett McConnell University and Berry College. At Truett McConnell, he was voted team Captain, a Captain's award winner, and Co-MVP. At Berry College, he was a two-time Conference Champion and received the Most Improved College Male Player award by the Coosa Valley Tennis Association in his senior year. His overall collegiate record was 105 wins and 45 losses. In his playing after college, he earned a #1 ranking in doubles and a #6 ranking in singles in the state of Georgia. In 2016, he was named "Tennis Pro of the Year" by Best Self Atlanta Magazine. Rob still enjoys competing and plays at the AA level of ALTA, which is the world's largest tennis league. He has been a speaker and presenter for the USPTA Georgia Chapter, as well as a college consultant for several colleges. He is a certified Cardio Tennis Instructor, a longtime member of the Wilson Advisory Staff, and a Special Olympics volunteer. In 2015, he created the Wilson Challenge, a men's tournament that has grown in popularity in the Metro Atlanta area. Rob has also produced over 100 videos on YouTube. You can follow him on YouTube under Rob Carver Tennis and contact him at robcarver@bellsouth.net.

1) Cross court consistency over winners

2) mix it up, don't stay in one position keep them guessing

3) Know where to strike, be aware for all weaknesses

4) first service ball in

5) communicate

6) get to the net

7) be alert @ net
keep active in a
more around, fake
poach just don't stand
there.

8) Move your feet

9) visualize

10) make opponents hit weak
shots, set up partner to
volley and put away

11) never give up on a point

12) target middle

13) hit groundstrokes deep

14) hit the ball where you are
standing back-back front-front

15) Your job @ the back is not to win the point there set up net

16) agressive net player every now & than go down the line 1 out of 10 times)

17) low volley at net hit to base line

18) getting a lob backside both people get to service line

19) your at the net your partner serves and the reciever lobs over you go back to no man's land get ready

20) when you lob opponet both partners need to get your toes to the service line, see #18

Approving poach

1st step footwork)
left foot step forward
split step ready to move
or pulse forward
little steps + than
go towards net strap

Go to ball, don't wait
No lateral movements
Take a step toward
mid net strap

CPSIA information can be obtained
at www.ICGtesting.com
Printed in the USA
BVHW041345140422
634332BV00016B/863

9 781665 303538